EVENTOLOGY.

EVENTOLOGY®

THE SCIENCE BEHIND NONPROFIT FUNDRAISING

DARREN DIESS, BAS
MICHELLE GILMORE, CFRE

Requests for permission to make copies of any part of the work should be emailed to the following address: hello@fundraisingadvisors.org.

www.fundraisingadvisors.org

Published and distributed by Merack Publishing

Library of Congress Control Number: 2019938774
Diess, Darren, 1967 -
Gilmore, Michelle, 1968 -

(Hard cover) ISBN 978-1-949635-17-1
(Perfect bound) 978-1-949635-18-8

Cover Concept by Jimi Scherer

Interior layout and design by Yvonne Parks

Printed in the United States of America

DEDICATION

This book is dedicated to the helpers of the world.
May these teachings help you to reach your full potential.

CONTENTS

ACKNOWLEDGMENTS

Darren

I dedicate this book to the many mentors and clients that have trusted me along the way. From the first conversation I had with Paul when he suggested I embark on this journey within the auction industry, to the first time I took the stage at an event, the sense of purpose that came from working with Kim and Rachel from Rotary and the guidance I have received from many of my industry connections and personal friends. I thank my family, my mom, my wife Joie, daughters Alyssa and Caitlyn and my son Daniel, all for supporting me and putting up with me during this process.

I'm sorry my Dad did not get to see this book, he was excited when we started this almost 3 years ago.

Michelle

This book is dedicated to those who have lifted me, taught me, tolerated me, granted me with grace and have gifted me with their love. Thank you Ted, Tyler, Travis, Tucker, my dad, George, and my sweet mother, Melody, who would be very proud of this and me. My sister Marilyn and her namesake, my Aunt Marilyn, who believed in my journey and success, thank you and I love you. The original inspiration to teach and learn to teach was given to me by a number of important teachers in my life. I am thankful for each and every one of them.

PREFACE

The beauty of holding a fundraising event is that in the act of gathering your constituents—your sponsors, donors, and even beneficiaries—you are creating a powerful community around your organization. As a result, when people receive your annual fund letter, they'll think not only of you and the value your organization brings, but how *they* play a part in it. They will be moved to continue their annual contribution. A well-executed fundraising event creates a ripple effect within the community. It gives board members an opportunity to invite and engage their circle of influence and participate in stewardship. Events build meaningful friendships, create opportunities for newcomers, providing volunteers a way to get involved when they may not be normally inclined to do so. The impact is far-reaching and serves a purpose beyond that of simply fundraising, so it's essential to get it right.

This book will help you do just that.

As co-authors we bring to the table two vastly different perspectives. To begin with, we're a man and a woman, so that alone creates a difference in opinion. But we also approach nonprofit fundraising from totally opposite angles. One of us, Michelle, is a CFRE (Certified Fund Raising Executive) and a Senior Development Director of a large multinational nonprofit organization who thinks about fundraising from an Executive Director's position, taking into consideration what the board will say, what donors will say, and what will or won't fly in the nonprofit world. The other of us, Darren, is a BAS (Benefit Auctioneer Specialist), who looks at fundraising through a totally different set of eyes; that of a showman. Every event is a production, we want to make sure we put on a memorable, over-the-top show. What can be done to yield the highest return on investment and help a nonprofit gain the maximum amount of funds to create a significant impact in their community? These two different perspectives when combined into one book create a unique and immensely powerful tool, because it allows you as the nonprofit professional to be able to think holistically and take both sides into consideration when planning your fundraising efforts.

Despite our differences in opinion, one thing we absolutely agree on 100% of the time is that managing fundraising well is a marathon and not a sprint. It is short-sighted and leaves an immense amount of money on the table if you're only viewing your organization's fundraising efforts as a single annual event and a year-end campaign. Your event may get the glory and be positioned as the most important feature in your fundraising program, but truth be told, it is managing the days, weeks, and months before and after an event well that makes all the difference.

In *Eventology*, our goal is to provide you with a step-by-step guide to serve as a road map to help you through those days, weeks, and months leading up to and following the creation and execution of a well-run and wildly financially successful fundraising event.

There is a science to fundraising. There are predictable formulas that—when followed—will yield the results you so desperately desire.

Throughout this book, we'll provide you with the resources necessary to put on a successful fundraiser so you can further your mission, bring in the revenue to sustain your important work, and build meaningful long-term relationships with your donors and the community. You'll be equipped with the tools and knowledge to maximize any type of event—from a golf tournament to a high-end gala. From volunteer management and procuring auction items to post-event stewardship, the practical guidance you'll gain in this book will empower you to turn your event "guests" into advocates for your organization and long-time donors for years to come. Consider this book your ultimate source for everything you need to know to be effective in your fundraising endeavors.

Let's dive in.

Darren & Michelle

CHAPTER 1
THE HIDDEN COST
OF TRADITION

"Oh, no, we can't do that," said Joan, the Executive Director of a prospective nonprofit client in my initial meeting with her and her benefit auction ("Gala") committee. I had just made the suggestion to eliminate the silent auction at their fall fundraising event as a means to cut down volunteer time and fatigue and help increase event profit. She shut me down. "People love the silent auction. Many of our guests attend just to shop. Plus, the board will never approve it. This is our signature event. People attend with certain expectations. We can't make such a drastic change—not this year."

Joan, in her tenth year as Executive Director, "knew her board's expectations and apt for change." She knew that it was a challenge to get them to participate and embrace their fundraising role with the events even as they were. She also understood what attendees of the event had grown accustomed to. "Our guests are trained," she said. (Yes, she really did say that). However, she had a big problem on her hands. Within the last three years, event attendance had slipped dramatically, staff turnover had reached an all-time high, and the volunteer event chairs were so burned out that not only did many of them refuse to return as chairs, they left the board and swore off the event entirely. Something needed to change fast for the sake of this year's event.

In my interview with Joan and her team, I listened intently to their concerns and challenges. After learning they had 425 guests and over 120 silent auction items, I explained that often times the silent auction brings results that are 40 to 60% of retail value. I made the bold suggestion to consider removing the silent auction altogether or moving it to an online opportunity and instead explore more lucrative fundraising options. Joan's hesitant response made it clear to me that this organization was entrenched in the tradition of the way things had always been done. After probing a bit more, I learned that one of the distinctive features of the fall event was an *open bar*. There was theoretically no ceiling on this cost component of the event. Rather than suggesting they eliminate the open bar entirely, I offered a thought to host 300 people rather than the customary 425. I was met with equal resistance. "Only 300 people? We need as many people as possible to reach our fundraising goal for the night!" Joan shifted in her chair. As an alternative, I hinted that it may be a good idea to host drinks for the first hour of the evening and then transition to a cash bar. They could also consider giving each attendee two drink tickets. Joan's eyes darted over to her two staff members and then back to me. "Our guests love a party, the open bar is a must," she said firmly. After a pause she added, "And by the way, we HAVE to increase our revenue this year."

If you have experience in fundraising, this story may sound all too familiar. As meaningful as traditions are, they come with a cost in nonprofit environments. Some traditions can hold you back in a competitive and evolving fundraising market. Technology and shifting societal demographics demand evolution and innovative approaches. As the number of fundraising events continues to rise, so does the competition for donor dollars. Staying relevant in this changing environment and catering to our fast-paced, distracted, multitasking society is not just a best practice for nonprofits, it's a matter of survival.

The "safety" in tradition was costing Joan's organization in ways she and her team had not considered. The fear of making changes was holding them back from success. Sure, the idea of making changes that would maximize spending and impact was a difficult pill for Joan to swallow, but it was one she would not regret. After further discussions and reviewing case studies from previous clients, I was able to show Joan that some simple adjustments to the event structure could make a significant impact on the organization's net revenue. Better yet, I was able to convince her to bring the proposed changes to the board. I worked through each objection that she had and showed her the vision for a donor-centric event. Joan, and eventually the board, came to understand that attendees who were coming to the event to get stuff for pennies on the dollar were not really there to support the organization's mission—they were there to get a deal. The nonprofit would be better off to send those people to the swap meet and bring in people who were sold on the mission and were ready to support it with their money.

The end result was a complete transformation. The board approved the new event format and guests flocked to the event and spent like never before. By making strategic changes in the event's run of show, revenue streams, and mission messaging, individual donations that night increased over the previous year by 30%. The fundraiser was a sold out event and became a hot ticket in years to follow. The volunteer event chair even returned to her post.

BOARD BUY IN

Joan's concern that her board would object to change is not a unique situation. Knowing how to address those concerns is key to increasing revenue, building your organization's reach and keeping volunteers and donors engaged with your mission. It's time for nonprofits to really dig deep into the science and the formulas behind their traditions. Many organizations need to recognize that the *bottom line* (net revenue) of events includes the expense of the time it takes to pull off a successful event plus hosting guests who may not spend any money. When all of those factors have been laid out and carefully examined, the need to try a new approach often presents itself clearly to the board.

Eventology suggests that you make this a board meeting activity. Take a close look at the data, review testimonials and then compare the results with past events, looking for patterns and trends. What have you done for the last three or four years? Take a close look at your planning and implementation and then start to test different scenarios to identify opportunities to do things differently. Pull the data from last year's silent auction, live auction and paddle raise and as a group do a deep dive into the numbers. When presented with the data and a direct comparison, it is easier to see when something is not a good use of time and money.

Next, have a brainstorming session where you can get board suggestions for new ideas and feedback on what you could improve on based on the numbers. Should we do an online auction? Should we scrap the silent auction and focus on just ten really great live items, what would the revenue look like if we did that? Pre-assign a few board members some research projects; for example, one member can look into online mobile options where guests can bid on their phones. Ask them to find out how much it costs, what the time associated in setting it up is, and how many volunteers you would need to run it. By creating a collaborative effort on the idea process, board member buy in becomes much easier to achieve.

In exploring all the options, we often come to the realization that we could do things a little differently yet experience big results and impact. It's not always necessary to make extreme changes. In Joan's situation we agreed on a great first step: changing the 120 silent items to 39 would increase revenue and lighten the load on the committee. Additional changes could be implemented the following year.

How can your nonprofit not only survive but thrive in your market? How can you stand out and be different? Making decisions on every level can significantly impact your next event.

CHAPTER 2
MINDSET - A NEW WAY OF THINKING

In order to overcome the hidden cost of tradition we must employ a new way of thinking.

This mindset is one based in opportunity, not fear.

Typically there are three types of fears present that hold people and nonprofits back from being able to fully step into this new way of operating:

- The Fear of The Ask
- The Fear of Not Looking Smart Enough (or not as Smart as Others)
- The Fear of Competition

Many board Presidents, Members and even Executive Directors of nonprofits experience some degree of discomfort when asking people they know to donate to their cause—especially if the individuals have already given so much. They don't want to ask volunteers, who have given so much of their time. Still others may be afraid to approach their friends and social contacts for donations because they feel they would be putting them out or making them feel pressured. Whatever the reason, and whatever the situation, we call this "The Fear of the Ask."

> **The Fear of the Ask is a close relative of The Fear of Selling.**

Often people's preconceived notions and assumptions get in their way. They equate asking for donations with selling, and position it in a negative light as if by making the request they're performing a disservice to their colleague, friend, or associate.

When we think about it rationally, we know that's not true, but in the moment it can be paralyzing.

All of these fears can be conquered with a simple shift in mindset.

If you can switch your mindset to the *provision of value*, then you're not selling. Being able to effectively share the story of the organization and connecting others to its purpose in a personally meaningful way to them is anything BUT selling. Rather, you're offering a unique opportunity for the person to get involved with an organization you believe in that's doing incredible things. We all know when we can become a part of something that's making a positive difference in the world, we feel amazing. You are offering an opportunity for them to be part of something that's really exciting and happening in their community—and attaching their name to it. They get to have ownership in something that's going to have an impact. You're not putting them out—you're supporting them in their ability to make a difference.

People really like to feel that they had a hand in making something special happen and feel good about their money making a difference. Getting the donor to feel amazing isn't just about creating feel-good emotions just for the fun of it, however; it's hard science that shows it's in our long term best interest to do so. A study conducted by Tristen K. Inagaki, Ph.D., and Lauren P. Ross at the University of Pittsburgh showed that "targeted support" like donating time or money to charities diminished brain activity in the amygdala, the part of the brain that is responsible for anxiety, PTSD and phobias when activated. "Humans thrive off social connections and benefit when they act in the service of others' well-being," according to the authors. As it turns out, the act of giving is scientifically proven to be good for our overall mental health!

When you have a fear of The Ask coming up, start with the low hanging fruit. It's easier to ask people for a gift who are already vested in your cause, which is why it's critical to develop relationships with your donors and keep them engaged. And it's also easier to ask someone for a contribution when they've given the year before. They've already acknowledged the value of your organization, they understand the work you do, and they are part of the mission. Volunteers, for instance, are naturally some of the first people to raise their hands with bids at galas and can become key contributors because they're so committed to the organization's success. They want to see the fruits of their labor. They are often times the easiest target audience to ask, but often they are the last ones to have been given the opportunity because fear holds people back from simply just asking the question.

THE FEAR OF NOT LOOKING SMART ENOUGH

We are at our best when we surround ourselves with greatness. But so many people fear that greatness around them may make them not look as smart, or that their ideas aren't as good as someone else's, or eliminate their ability to shine and be the hero.

The truth is that surrounding yourself with greatness actually does the opposite: it positions you as the leader, and separates you from the doers. Smart people make you look really, really GOOD. You want to surround yourself with as many savvy volunteers, vendors and as many great ideas as you possibly can, because that brings the level of success up for your organization and/or your event. Just as a musical conductor doesn't play an instrument but is typically credited with an orchestra's amazing success, such will be the case for you, too. The stronger your team and the more amazing they are, the better it reflects upon you as the leader.

And when it comes time for you to leave, the greatest legacy you can provide to the organization is a strong succession plan. The best way to ensure that happens isn't to make yourself the most powerful, smart person on the committee—it's to create and put in place a powerful team of rockstars who you simply LEAD and extract their best skills.

THE FEAR OF COMPETITION

We often see this within committees and with board/staff members—the perception that other people (even on the same team) are perceived as "competition."

Yes, even in the kind and caring nonprofit world it's not always bliss, holding hands and singing kumbaya around the campfire; the competitive instinct most definitely does exist.

Sometimes this happens internally among committee members, which we addressed above, and can be conquered by viewing others' brilliance as an asset and understanding that others' success is not a threat to yours.

Other times, however, it happens within the larger nonprofit community in a geographic area or between different individual nonprofit organizations.

One such way we see this manifest is when an organization tries to get their event on the calendar before another nonprofit's event so they can "beat them to the punch." They're trying desperately to get to the donor dollars first, and want to ask local businesses for support before another group gets to them. This becomes a challenge for not just you at the nonprofit level because it's so stressful, but it's also a challenge from a donor's perspective. A community leader and active donor may be invited to as many as 10 events in the fall. She sees the value of attending each and desires to support her fellow community members, but there are only so many Saturday nights—she will simply just have to pick and choose which organizations to support.

Consider setting aside the competitive nature that cripples nonprofits and invite the leadership of other NPOs and NGOs to join you around the table. Explore innovative ways to collaborate in your collective fundraising efforts. Rather than competing with each other, we invite you to change the narrative and leverage relationships to build community capacity and increase social impact. In the next chapter we'll discuss the idea further, and explore a fast growing concept known as "Collaborative Fundraising."

CHAPTER 3
COLLABORATIVE FUNDRAISING: 2 + 2 = 10

In his article, "Nonprofits: Do Not Be Afraid to Collaborate With One Another," Tom Hanley shares his take:

"When I mention 'collaboration' in meetings with other nonprofit directors, I can flip a coin on their reaction: will they cringe in disgust or light up like a light bulb. The overlying response can be summarized as: 'if I collaborate with another nonprofit, I risk losing a donor who learns about the work of another nonprofit. I'm not willing to help educate my donors and to help market other nonprofits to my donor base. It's too great a risk to my organization.'"

This competitive way of thinking and outlook is rooted in scarcity, and we hope you're the nonprofit director Tom mentions above who lights up like a light bulb at the mention of collaboration. If you're not, or if you have never explored this idea as a potential option for you and your organization, we invite you to consider this new way of thinking.

A CASE FOR COLLABORATION

There are 1.5 million nonprofits in the United States according to the National Center of Charitable Statistics. We're in the middle of a huge transfer of wealth as the Baby Boomer generation begins to hand off that wealth to the Gen Xers, and nonprofits are competing to be the beneficiary.

In our own community alone, there are over 162 fundraising events each year. Most NPOs currently host a gala, with goals ranging from $40,000 to $250,000. The average net from a gala is 50% to 65% of revenue. Combining the expenses around marketing, the venue, and third party vendors to host one large multi-organization event to impact a social need in our community could prove more profitable and change the face of philanthropy. In fact, local and national Family Foundations are pushing for nonprofits to work with other nonprofit partners in order to qualify for grant funding.

REAL LIFE EXAMPLE

Upon commencing work with a new NPO consulting client, we learned that their organization was competing with close to 800 events in their region during the three critical fundraising months of their season. They kept telling us, "We need to be better! Do more! Do things differently."

We began talking to the various organizations in the area about the idea of a collective of nonprofits coming together to put on one major event. All of them were head over heels about the idea! To do this we would need to impact the region (the "Valley," as we call it) in an area of greatest need. The focus became combating the homeless epidemic. Five nonprofits in the community working with the same population came together: a food pantry, a homeless shelter, an after-school outreach program, a medical clinic, and an employment resource center. They realized that with hosting their own individual fundraising events they were limited to their own invitees and sponsor lists, and for years they had been disappointed with the results. Thus the idea of "Five for Five" was born. Five causes with a goal of $5 million raised. The concept was simple: have one major blowout event to impact the Valley in a significant way, not just by alleviating homelessness but really ending the cycle of poverty and making such an impact that it could be clearly seen and identified in their community. Furthermore, it would create a model of change across the local philanthropic landscape, with the hope that it would create a ripple effect.

To make it work we needed the organizations to be on a level playing field; in order for it to be truly collaborative, everyone needed to be seen as an equal at the table. Once we could agree on this, we sat down and presented the concept to the leaders of the organizations. A collaborative effort was something that piqued their interest: they could see the potential for enormous impact in their community. Rather than asking people to donate a bit here and a bit there, a collaborative event gave them the opportunity to contribute to a "combined mission" with significant reach and impact.

SYNERGY: 2 + 2 = 10

Collaborative fundraising is an innovative way to garner support around a specific beneficiary target group. Bringing skill sets, volunteer enthusiasm, and passion for a cause together in one place exponentially increases the effectiveness of your results.

It's the concept of synergy… where the total equals more than the sum of the original parts.

As Jeffrey Walker states in his article, "Transitional Philanthropy: Leveraging Innovation to Build Sustainability," the idea that one nonprofit innovator will have the best model to scale falls flat when compared to integrating several great innovations from multiple sources into a collaborative network embedded in the larger social system. For example, a group of individuals who share a love of music were sad to see many music programs cut from public schools. Rather than start up a new nonprofit to bring music back to inner cities, they created the Quincy Jones Musiq Consortium to find ways to unify the 75 nonprofits from around the country already working on this issue.

Finding a way to combine the visions and resources of multiple organizations to execute a single mega-event where you bring all of the organizations' constituents together and host a fundraising event benefiting the shared cause or population, where the money gets split among the different nonprofits, is the ultimate definition of synergy. Let's face it: donors don't want to go to multiple events and write multiple checks. Let's make it easier for them to make an impact and feel good about it without having to go to event after event for the next number of weekends in a row.

COLLABORATIVE FUNDRAISING AT EVERY LEVEL

Collaborative fundraising isn't just for large NPOs who have the resources for a massive group event. It can also work *extremely* well for smaller nonprofits who don't have a large pool of people and resources to pull from. Take the example of our client who held two events per year: a fun run and a golf tournament that was hosted by a local realtor, of which they were the beneficiary. At our initial meeting to discuss their development plan and evaluate their events we quickly discovered a huge problem: they didn't have a donor database. The organization hadn't taken the time to capture contact information from past attendees or donors—there were no phone numbers, email addresses or donation records on file. Without that list of contacts to invite, planning a new event became exponentially more difficult.

We prompted them to start working with a like-organization from a neighboring community. The two organizations agreed to co-host a fundraising "walk for hunger" and pool their resources: time, money, volunteers and donors. By doing it this way, they were able to share the expenses and the money raised, which turned out to be an amount much greater than either nonprofit would have raised on their own. The event sponsors also saw this as a win; they got to write one check and received double the benefit by having their company promoted in two separate communities.

If you decide to give collaborative fundraising a try, look for other nonprofits where there is a connection. Look for what the common ground is while being mindful that there isn't too much commonality. You don't want to be serving the same community of people and sharing the same sponsors; it's critical that each organization can add new donors and new resources to the pool. Look at the big vision and who you want to service with your event and then reach out to other nonprofits that support that initiative through their own work.

As we continue to work with groups of nonprofit organizations, helping them to execute this concept through our own consulting practice, we see more and more results and greater impact and we believe wholeheartedly that this new way of thinking will truly change the landscape of event fundraising.

CHAPTER 4
THE ART & SCIENCE OF DELIVERING YOUR MESSAGE

People want to be part of something larger than themselves, and it's your duty to powerfully and effectively communicate what that "something" is.

The best way to do that is through the use of Mission and Impact Statements, creating an Impact Video, and Storytelling.

MISSION AND IMPACT STATEMENTS

The mission statement provides the purpose of the organization, where the outcome of its existence is succinctly described. If you're reading this book and are actively involved in the nonprofit world, you likely know your mission statement already. You know what it says, and you probably have it at the top of your website and the bottom of your letterhead. It's the driving force for program management and fundraising for your organization and it is (and should be) what the board considers when making any and all decisions.

Your mission—however important—is not what you use in day-to-day conversation. It's not read at events at the start of a speech or video, and it's not what board members rattle off when asked what type of organization they are volunteering for. Instead, that is the job of your 20 second impact statement or elevator pitch.

If you're a surgeon representing an international medical missions group, your message might sound something like this: "We're traveling the world to make a difference in children's lives—one scoliosis surgery at a time." Or perhaps your horse sanctuary utilizes abandoned race horses to provide therapeutic riding for autistic and special needs adults and children. Your message might be: "Turning tragedy into triumph: saving horses and improving lives."

PRO TIP

A terrific activity to conduct with the board at a board training, a group of volunteers you are training for an upcoming event, or the staff at a staff retreat is the 20 Second Impact Statement—Mad Lib Style. We kick off our *Eventology* workshops with this activity, and it is always amazing to see the engagement it creates.

Four things to remind your group when conducting this activity:

1. The 20 second impact statement you write MUST be unique to you and won't be the same as anyone else's impact statement within your organization. There is a single mission statement for the nonprofit that doesn't change from one stakeholder to another but is unique to the organization; the 20 second impact statement, on the other hand, *will* change from person to person and is unique to each stakeholder. You have your own why, and it's important to tap into your personal place of passion within the organization when doing this exercise.

2. This is meant to be something you will memorize: a flow of words that will come easily to you. Don't overthink it.

3. There are no right/wrong answers in this activity.

4. Practice your statement with a partner; even if it feels awkward and uncomfortable in the beginning, saying it out loud will help you refine and simplify it. It's like learning to play a new instrument—once you practice the chords over and over, you'll find a groove and it will sound so much more natural when you deliver it to people after you've practiced it a number of times.

20 SECOND IMPACT STATEMENT - MAD LIB STYLE

The first part of the twenty-second Impact Statement (the "Belief" statement) is intended to share your high-level vision and give a glimpse of your organization's values. The second part explains *what you do*. And the final part—the "Because" statement—tells the listener *why they should care*.

At _____, we believe_____

your organization's name and deeply held value

Every day we _____ for _____
verb - object constituents

the "Because" _____.
problem statement or opportunity statement

It may not seem very inspiring at first read, but, with some time and consideration, input from the group, and some careful editing, you'll have a solid 20 second Impact Statement that can really pack a punch.

Here are two examples of different 20 second Impact Statements:

At Outdoor Adventures, we believe nature changes the course of a life.

We lead the field by counseling, coaching, and funding outdoor educators and thought-leaders.

Every day we ensure as many youth as possible can partake in the life-changing experience of the outdoors.

*(**The because**) We improve the lives of youth today and create dynamic outdoor stewards for tomorrow.*

***At Ride-A-Bus to the Arts**, we believe field study opportunities provide life-changing experiences for public school children.*

***Everyday we** do our best to fund buses for field study trips for K-12 public school children in budget-restricted school districts and lower socio-economic neighborhoods where these are not available.*

*(**The because**) The youth of today are the artists, musicians, dancers, scientists and leaders of tomorrow.*

These messages are designed to introduce, inspire, and intrigue. Armed with a sure-fire way to clearly communicate the big vision of your organization, you'll never again be faced with that crippling feeling of not knowing what to say when someone asks what you do. As a result, you'll play an important part in influencing your organization's brand (or reputation) and ensuring that your listener has a clear idea of why your organization matters.

Get creative and have some fun with this exercise!

IMPACT VIDEO

A brief impact video is very useful in illustrating your mission statement. It's most important to have the people whose lives have been changed by the generosity of the donations in the video so donors can understand that they actually can really and truly make a difference. It's not just the Executive Director talking about what the organization is going to do, or a doctor or clinician speaking about the research behind the program's efficacy. At the event, your job is to take care of your *donor*. So put the smiling kids in the video, or the happy, playful puppies or the proud new graduates; illustrate the impact, and make the viewer *feel good*.

Many people think that creating an impact video is not cost effective, and may not be budget-friendly. This is absolutely something you can do, even on a shoestring budget. You can shoot the footage yourself; sometimes the most raw and real, emotional clips are what grab the attention of your donors the most. It doesn't need to be perfectly polished (though it *is* a wise investment to leaving the editing part of the process to a professional).

Remember—your video should be both poignant and to the point so that your audience quickly understands the need and readily heeds the call to action. It should tell the story. And you can utilize the video in a lot of different places after you've revealed it for the very first time at your fundraising event: on social media, in an email introducing a new donor, staff member, or volunteer to the organization for the first time, at the beginning of a donor meeting—the possibilities are endless.

PRO TIP
2 minutes or less!

You're fighting for people's attention in an attention deficit society. We can laugh out loud or be brought to tears with a 30 second commercial on Super Bowl Sunday, so don't be concerned about only having 2 minutes to tell your story or share the impact you're making every day. Use your 2 minutes wisely. Script the storyline, test it out and watch people's reactions to see if it touches them as deeply as you want it to, and find inspiring and moving music that evokes emotion in the viewer.

Whether you spend a lot or a little on it, a killer impact video is an important tool because it's something you create once but can utilize over and over again. It isn't just an expense line item—it's an expense that will actually *make* you money.

STORYTELLING

Storytelling is what connects the nonprofit organization with their donors. How are we going to make people sit up, take notice, and engage with us? It is through the story you tell them about your organization: it's mission, the problem you are addressing, and how they are an integral part of the solution.

When telling the story, the goal is to make the hair on their arms raise. You want your audience to *feel* the emotions of the story. In his keynote speech, "The Art of Storytelling," Matthew Luhn, one of the original Pixar members of the writing team that created ToyStory, describes the five elements of an impactful story:

1. The Hook
2. Life-Changing Content
3. Connecting with the Right Crowd
4. Authenticity
5. Structure

Including all of these elements will create a story that inspires and compels your audience to feel—and ideally give. In his speech, he continues: "When we all learned how to write a story in school, we learned the story model with setting, characters, plot, problem and finally the solution." If you're selling a product, however, to hook your audience or connect the crowd to your organization, you need to do more. You need to bring your guests up emotionally and then down; then up again, and then down; this roller coaster of emotions takes your guests on a journey with your organization and those served by the organization.

When you can craft the story in such a way that it empowers them as the audience members—when you can show that their gift of $100 or $100,000 is everything and you can't do it without them—that's really both powerful and magical.

THE DELIVERY

There is a science to delivering your message at a fundraising event. The number of times the message is delivered, the sequence of delivery, length of time, and even the number of presenters all are factors in the successful and compelling delivery of your organization's impact.

Using a well planned and executed strategy to communicate your organization's purpose can drive home the critical importance of your mission. Offer your message repeatedly to your guests throughout the event by utilizing different storytelling vehicles (a video presentation, personal experience speeches, images, and infographics on your accomplishments) to successfully pull on the heart strings and open the wallets of your guests.

When it comes to delivering the event's signature impact story, there are three important questions to ask:

- How do you choose who is going to tell the story? Is it going to be a paid emcee, a fundraising auctioneer (who is a professional storyteller), or is it going to be somebody who knows one of the recipients really well: a good friend or a family member—a mother, daughter, grandmother?

- How will the signature story be told? Is it a video story that will be shown, or is the story going to be told/delivered live? Telling a story in person allows the people attending the fundraiser to make a one-to-one connection with the cause. Having the person who has benefited from the cause present—telling the story him/herself—holds so much more weight and resonates with the crowd at a deeper level because it's tangible. It's real. They can feel the passion, the emotion, the connection. And you can enhance all of these things with sound, lighting, and creating a very special energy and buzz in the room which provides a memorable experience that will stay with your guests in the days and weeks that follow.

- Who is the audience? In our pitch, we have to make a case that the donors will love. We could have a great story, but if it's geared towards millennials and most of the donors in the room are baby boomers, the story may end up being less impactful than it could be. We have to know who's in the room, why they're there, and then build the story using that as the base. The story may well need to be changed from an evening gala to an afternoon Rotary meeting, because it might be an entirely different demographic and environment. The facts will be the same, but the way the story is told and the way it connects to the audience needs to be able to be customized to suit the donor landscape—the ones listening to the story at that particular event.

Once you have the answers to the three main questions above, there are some additional important questions to answer next:

- If it's an in person delivery, has the storyteller memorized the narrative or are they reading it?

- If live, are you using a high quality sound system? (If so, you MUST allow time to practice 3-4 times—*at the venue with the A/V team, on the exact sound system you'll be using*—before the presentation).

- Can all members of the audience clearly see the speaker without obstruction? Is the speaker elevated (ie. on a stage) or positioned in a way where everyone in the audience can both see and hear them clearly? (If not, change whatever you need to in order to ensure this is the case).

- Is it being streamed/is virtual attendance an option? If so, is the video being captured and streamed in such a way that remote audience members can see and hear just as well as the people present in the room?

- What happens when the person reading or telling their story doesn't show up to the event due to a family emergency or worse?

AVOID THIS!
A note from Darren

At a recent event, John, the board president, mentioned that he would like to speak briefly at the top of the program and share the impact of their organization to the crowd before we did the paddle raise. Typically, I like to rehearse this well in advance, but since I was about to take the stage, I reluctantly agreed. The mission impact video played, and the crowd was quiet and engaged. They were focused and ready to give. As the video ended I walked on stage, and up came John. I handed him the microphone and he said, "Folks, we have been asking and asking and we aren't at our goal yet. The board has sent emails, the staff sent a letter, we have been asking businesses and working as hard as we can, anything you can give will get us to the finish line. Please help us out." What John did was make it all about him. All about the board and staff. He took away the precious moments we had after the heartwarming video where the donors could feel their emotions calling them to stand up and be the change, and replaced it with his personal plea. Going away from the mission cost John and his organization that day, and it can happen to anyone without even them realizing the damage they've done.

As an organization, you need to spotlight the things that matter. While admirable, focusing on your team working their butts off to raise money is far less captivating than the feel-good story of someone's life you've been able to impact.

PLEASE resist the urge to shift the focus and make it about you and your organization and instead keep the focus on the donor, and let THEM be the hero.

When you've reached someone's heart, you've appealed to them. They've heard you. You've said something that has connected with them in a profound way. This is the moment when many will be compelled to become part of the solution with their donation.

This is where the giving process begins.

CHAPTER 5
DIFFERENT
TYPES OF GIVING

We often speak to organizations that want to host a large gala because, "a fellow community organization just hosted their gala, and it brought in $250,000," for example. Large scale events come with large scale budgets. What they didn't hear about is the $100,000 budget it took to put on the event, the hundreds of volunteer hours it took to execute, and the percentage of their staff's time that was involved in planning and putting on the event. In fact, if staff and volunteer hours were factored into the budget, that same event might have yielded a less than satisfactory net return.

Events *can* be an effective form of fundraising—if scaled to your organization's size, audience and mission. But as technology continues to evolve with new solutions to streamline processes and ease fundraising, non-event fundraising, can—in many cases—be more successful in terms of return on investment (ROI).

In this chapter, we'll go through the different types of giving, weigh in with the pros and cons for each type, and help you determine what fundraising vehicle will serve your nonprofit best based on your mission, who your target donors are, and the size of your organization.

EVENT-BASED GIVING

As an auctioneer, I've witnessed a single event create a community. With an effective story that brings guests together emotionally, a group of guests at an event form a bond and a subconscious mission to make a difference for the beneficiaries of the organization. Honestly, you never know who may be impacted at your event and what lasting impact they, in turn, may have on your organization. You may gain a key volunteer or board member, a new sponsor, or even a legacy donor.

Applying the Eventology Method to the different types of events below will help to maximize return and make your guest experience the number one priority.

Gala

PROS: Galas are a perfect platform to celebrate a milestone, wrap up a year-long campaign, or generate buzz in the community for your organization. They can bring large groups of people together to fundraise in one night and they allow you to expand your audience and donor base. Sponsorship opportunities provide local businesses and corporations wanted exposure and recognition and can be a significant portion of your event revenue.

CONS: Expensive to execute. Taxing on staff and volunteers. Can get stale when done the same way year after year.

EVENTOLOGY RECOMMENDATIONS: Provide the opportunity to pre-register and pre-bid on auction items (online auction vs. silent). Greet guests upon arrival with champagne/sparkling water, assign dedicated board members to greet and accompany key guests into the venue until they have connected with a person or group.

Athletic/Endurance Event

(Fun Run, 5K, Walk, Cycling, Walk a thon)

PROS: Attracts successful, ambitious people who are typically philanthropic by nature. Great way to gather contact information for future donor solicitations. Budget-friendly in terms of expenses, especially with dedicated volunteers who can source in-kind donations to cover hard costs.

CONS: Donations from participants are typically low. Can be difficult to build large event due to highly competitive field. Registrants may participate for reasons other than supporting your organization. Many one time gifts with little conversion to monthly or lifetime supporters.

EVENTOLOGY RECOMMENDATIONS: Brand and an engaging theme are key. Only spend marketing dollars on trackable digital media and advertising channels that can provide lead generation. Use core donor base as an honorary planning committee and offer pledge-based giving programs with incentives.

Golf Tournament

PROS: A feel good, business networking event which can be great for fundraising. Corporate sponsorship opportunities for golf tournaments often bring in larger amounts than other events and can be extremely beneficial to both organization and corporate sponsors in terms of visibility.

CONS: With a lunch or dinner this can make for a long day. Participants are mainly guests of a sponsor with no affiliation to the organization. Some golfers may feel their fee to play is all they can afford to give.

EVENTOLOGY RECOMMENDATIONS: 18 (tee) + 18 (hole) = 36 sponsors (green fees are not included) will make it a profitable event. Are you considering a fundraising auction? Silent auction/ASK? Golf events can offer a great return when planned correctly and when they focus on the why of the organization. Most golf tournaments have 100 to 144 golfers lined up and ready to make a difference at the 9 AM tee time, so set up the golfers around the putting green, do your welcome announcements, and explain how the funds raised will make a difference. Conduct the live auction right then and there. Add Bid numbers on the back of the scorecard for an extra dose of awesome.

Carnival/Concert/Festival

PROS: These bring families and younger audiences to events, and are an excellent source for recruiting volunteers. They provide a good opportunity to educate the audience about your mission with an information booth give-away. This is good for many small gifts (ie. coin collections, tip jars, game tickets, etc.).

CONS: Budget for these events can be heavy on front-loaded expenses. Profitability is reliant on ticket sales and food/swag sales, and rain or extreme heat is unpredictable and can spoil success.

EVENTOLOGY RECOMMENDATIONS: Pre-sell tickets at an early-bird rate. Drive ticket sales through paid channels, online and social media. Spend money on event software and an event planner, especially if yours is a volunteer-run organization. The venue is key, so make it all about donor experience: parking, shuttles, ease of entry, sound quality, and safety.

Breakfast Fundraiser

PROS: The breakfast crowd is an ideal fundraising audience. Typically retirees with time on their hands who are in no rush to leave, these people are often philanthropically-minded and are there because they're interested in what you do. Also great for the business crowd, the early day usually presents minimal (or fewer) distractions. Make sure to have GOOD coffee on hand!

CONS: Annual breakfast events need to have a draw to keep engagement; they can lose steam and attendance if done at the same location with the same program each year.

EVENTOLOGY RECOMMENDATIONS: Offer a low ticket price to cover the cost of breakfast (the least expensive meal to purchase). Invite guests who donated a certain amount or more the year prior and offer them free tickets. Engage the audience with raffle prizes, door prizes and games.

Lunch & Learn/Behind the Scenes Tour/Open House/Grand Opening

PROS: By far the best way for your donors or prospects to see and learn what you do, who you serve, and experience how their funds are being spent. It's a good way to connect high-end donors with decision makers/leaders in an organization or community. Lunch and learns are excellent for recruiting teams, walkers/riders for endurance events.

CONS: Direct ROI is low. For example, there is no direct ask at a standard lunch and learn or behind-the-scenes tour. The costs associated with these are considered an investment in future fundraising and stewardship of current donors. You cannot always predict what guests will see on a behind-the-scenes tour, so there's a little bit of risk with this option.

EVENTOLOGY RECOMMENDATIONS: Invite a mix of veteran donors/volunteers and prospective donors to your lunch and learn, and host and publicize a VIP guest (mayor, superintendent, surgeon). Add small windows of time where guests will be able to engage with each other, and have a less formal presentation. Create a plan/put a goal in place to get 3 to 5 meetings set up with new donors from the event, but be cautious when making an ask in these situations.

REAL LIFE EXAMPLE
A note from Michelle

An exception to the rule? Each year my organization hosted four behind-the-scenes tours, mainly as a stewardship opportunity for donors. We made it a practice not to make a direct ask, mainly because these were post-gift acknowledgment activities. At one tour at the public middle school, shortly following a large fundraiser a month prior, we were showcasing the funding in classrooms to some of our largest donors and school administrators. There were 15 people on the tour and we spent two hours with the principal as our tour guide. Each teacher welcomed us and asked the students to share what they were doing with the funds provided by this group of guests and our organization. The tour attendees were extremely impressed. At the culminating breakfast the Executive Director thanked everyone who attended and mentioned that we were so close to hitting our goal with our recent fundraiser, and if they knew someone who had yet to donate, please share the experience of the day with them. One gentleman asked, "How close are you?" She said, "$10,000." He said, "I'll put up a third, how about you Dave?" Dave said, "Yes, I'm in for a third." The rest of the group all chipped in, and in five short minutes we raised $10,000 to reach our goal for the campaign.

Private Party/Foodie Event/Cocktail Party

PROS: Can be a great replacement for a gala to avoid the expense of venue and food costs that are associated with a large scale gala. A well-planned, themed event at a "must-see" home or gallery can bring in thousands of dollars for your cause. A chef dinner/wine talk/dessert demonstration offers exclusive opportunities that intrigue invitees.

CONS: Fundraising is heavily reliant on the program. Unlike sponsored events, while underwriting may help defray costs, the majority of funds raised will come from guests on the night of the event. The program should be tailored directly to the audience inspiring how support for the cause will make a radical impact. Storytellers / speakers should be invested, respected, and trusted by those who are attending—well rehearsed and very compelling. One should not "just wing it" here. Practice the perfect pitch repeatedly, yet be sure to keep it real, honest and very transparent. Focus on the mission, how you can make change, help, or lead the future. Crafted with a very compelling "Give/ASK", it's a simple formula that is typically successful.

EVENTOLOGY RECOMMENDATIONS: Spend an extra amount of time planning the arrival of guests. Offer valet parking, have your guests be welcomed by a VIP host/hostess, and include a formal check-in. Provide name tags for guests; the increased comfort level will encourage a more social atmosphere. Have a "lead gift" arranged in advance and make it easy for guests to make a donation. Very important: be sure to have an appropriate sound system! Everyone in the room should be able to clearly hear everyone who will be speaking. It may only be one large speaker that you need, but you should NEVER have to yell or raise your voice.

Telethon/Radio-a-thon

PROS: The MDA telethon, hosted by Jerry Lewis from 1966 to 2010 before he stepped down, raised over 2.4 billion dollars over that time. Telethons and radio-thons have been a mainstay of fundraising and still have great potential when brought to the present digital age. They are most successful in a small area—either a small town or a small community of followers/friends/fans. Social media and online giving make fundraising and collecting pledges pain-free.

CONS: It takes an exorbitant amount of planning time and resources to make this type of event successful. Live acts/performances mixed with video clips and interviews make production extremely consuming. As such, the cost associated with media time and talent can be prohibitive to the success of this event.

EVENTOLOGY RECOMMENDATIONS: Limit the time-frame for the campaign with clear benchmarks for giving and matching gifts. For example, this hour every donation made will be matched dollar for dollar by Super Smile Dentistry. Offer multiple ways to give: by mail, online donations, mobile giving, social media campaigns, and by phone. 80% of the goal should be raised before the event in sponsors, gifts and pledges. The BIG show should be a celebration!

NON-EVENT GIVING

We'll give you a brief rundown here, but you can Google each of these concepts to learn more if you care to; they're important, but given the name of the book, our focus here is on events, so this will simply be a light overview.

Recurring Giving

If you are looking to increase donor retention rates and lifetime giving levels with smaller investments, recurring giving may be for you. Recurring giving has the highest ROI in fundraising: the cost to provide a recurring giving program and sustain the revenue is the lowest per dollar spent.

Workplace Giving

Workplace giving is where employees have the opportunity to donate funds to your organization through a payroll deduction. Often through matching gifts or volunteer work programs, an additional sum goes to your organization.

Planned Giving

Planned giving involves any type of giving to your organization by individuals in which plans for that act of giving need to be made in advance. For example, say a long time supporter of your causes passes away, they would be able to bequest some of their estate (known as "estate giving") to your organization if they so choose, or part of their 401K or even their life insurance. All they would need to do is plan this out ahead of time, make sure it is in their will, and follow the proper legal procedures to solidify the eventual gift.

The two most popular forms of planned giving are arguably Charitable Giving and Grant Giving.

Annuity/Legacy Giving is a type of planned giving that can greatly benefit both the donors and your organization. In essence, it involves a simple contract that is drawn up between your organization and the donor. Then, the donor will gift a large sum of money (usually no less than $25,000, though donors have been known to donate estates and other valuables, as well). In return for this donation, the donor will be able to claim an income charitable tax deduction, and will receive a stipend from the organization each month until they pass away. Then, when the donor passes away, your organization is "gifted" the remainder of the donation, to do with as they see fit.

Endowment Giving

According to Joe Garecht from *The Fundraising Authority* in his article, "Successful Endowment Fundraising", an endowment is a pool of funds raised by a nonprofit organization which can then be invested. The proceeds provide returns or ongoing income to the nonprofit, either for a designated purpose or for general operating support.

CROWDFUNDING

Crowdfunding is on track to be a $300 billion dollar business by 2025. Although originally developed to attract business investors to entrepreneurial startups, it is now widely used in the nonprofit world. Based on the premise that it "takes a village," an individual or organization can post a project or cause on a crowdfunding website and donors will contribute to the cause. Go Fund Me launched in 2010 and has brought in $5 billion dollars itself, edging out up-and-coming competitors like Kickstarter and Indiegogo. Having multiple players in the field has not only led the cost to drop significantly for the licensing of these solutions, but the percentage the host company takes has now decreased as well, making this a viable option for non profit organizations of all sizes.

PEER-TO-PEER FUNDRAISING

Peer-to-Peer fundraising sometimes gets put into the same category as Crowdfunding, but it has some clear distinctions. The idea is the same as Crowdfunding in that you're asking many people to donate to a single cause utilizing a social platform. The difference however, is that in Peer-to-Peer fundraising your supporters directly reach out to their own network of friends, family, and business associates and personally ask them to participate in the cause. Perfect for sports teams, schools and endurance events that call for pledges, small targeted amounts to fund equipment, programs costs, trainer hours, art teacher's supplies, etc., this type of fundraising has low overhead and low manpower requirements in terms of volunteers.

CHAPTER 6
PEOPLE—YOUR MOST IMPORTANT ASSET

In science, all things are made of atoms. In the world of fundraising, your people are your atoms. Without them, NPOs would neither exist, nor thrive. People are your biggest asset and they are the building blocks of a truly successful organization. This chapter takes a look at the five key groups of people for all nonprofits (Donors, Board Members, Volunteers, Sponsors, and Vendors) and gives insight on how best to find them, manage them and most importantly INSPIRE them to get and stay involved with your organization.

DONORS

Finding donors is not an easy task, but taking the time to investigate who your donors *really are* will make it much simpler to find more of them and bring them on board with your organization.

This is vital, because when asking donors to give to your cause, you absolutely must use the right messaging and language. In order to do so, you first must truly understand who your audience is. We mentioned this before when talking about your mission statement and impact video, but it's worth reiterating: while the information stays the same, you need to deliver it differently depending on whether you're addressing a group of Millennials or a room full of Baby Boomers with potentially the same (or more) capacity to donate. You have to tailor your ask to drive your message home to different donor groups.

YOUR DONOR AVATAR

It's one thing to describe who you *think* your donors are. But spending the time to uncover not just who you think they are, but who the DATA *says they are,* will be an enormous asset to your nonprofit.

This begins with the development of what we call your "Donor Avatar". This will become your Ideal Donor profile, with the hallmarks and attributes that the data tells you is associated with your target donor's persona.

The process is relatively simple to develop your nonprofit's Donor Avatar. Begin by using your donor management software to run a report of all of your donors, ranking them from most to least by financial contribution. Let's say you have 500 donors on your list. Take a look at your top 100 and sort them in to A, B and C lists using the following criteria. Your A's will be those donors who donate a lot AND are a pleasure to deal with. They're your rockstar donors. If you could clone them and make every donor just like them you'd be on top of the world. Your C's are the opposite. They may donate generously, but can be notoriously difficult to communicate with or offer some other challenge as a donor. They're the ones that make you cringe when you see their name in your inbox or pop up on your caller ID. For those donors in your Top 100 list who you aren't really sure if they're an A or a C, add them to your B list.

Now take your A list and begin profiling them with whatever touchpoints you might already have: zip code, gender, age, etc. Once you've completed the profile with what already exists, start to look at other touchpoints to add to the list. Examine not just their demographics, but add some psychographics to the list as well. Once you have some criteria to analyze, begin to look for the pattern that will undoubtedly emerge. Is it geographic? Is it their employment type? Maybe they all drive the same brand of car? Take that pattern and apply it to your remaining donors numbered 101-500, looking for rockstars. You likely will find a number of potential A donors waiting in the wings. And once you know who your true A-listers are, keep profiling them. Pay attention to the referral source or person who brought them into the organization. Any pattern there? Begin to treat the A's like the VIPs they are. Talk to them personally and find out exactly how they like to communicate with you. By phone? Email? Text? Cater to their personal preferences, and keep track of them in your donor management software. See if there are any additional patterns or trends in this information, too.

FINDING NEW DONORS

Whether you are just starting out or you're looking to grow your existing database, finding new donors can feel like a daunting task. Here are five pathways we believe are proven and effective ways of getting new donors on board:

1. Remember, like attracts like. By identifying who your A-list donors are when you developed your Donor Avatar, you can source organic leads through referrals from your existing A-listers who most certainly know other A's who could become new donors for your organization.

2. Put out an open invitation to participate in a non-monetary way (ie. volunteer opportunities). This will help you find people with a philanthropic mindset and/or values, and chances are high that they will in turn invite friends who also share the same mindset.

3. Utilize free or inexpensive tools to reach out to your community. For example, find a local newspaper or online magazine who would be willing to share one of your amazing stories of hope and overcoming obstacles. Insert your organization's name in as many times as possible to connect your mission to the story. This shouldn't be a direct plug for your nonprofit, simply a really great feel good story that you are a part of.

4. Reach out to like-minded nonprofits and invite them to attend your event. Some nonprofits may even be willing to share your mission and event with their donor pool.

5. Examine your current list of donors and determine whether they are all still active donors. Your next top donor may (likely) already be in your database, yet no one has reached out to him/her—beyond just random invitations and the odd newsletter here and there, that is—to make an ask outright. Work on maximizing and optimizing your current donors and donor database before spending a lot of time looking for new ones.

GIVING CIRCLES

A way to draw in new donors and keep existing ones is to designate different donor groups—typically by giving levels. These create opportunities for your organization to identify donors and acknowledge their giving in a public way. While all contributions will be published and acknowledged in your donor materials, there are only exclusive benefits at the top two or three levels so that you're not driving yourself crazy as an organization trying to create brand new and different benefits for all of these levels.

Another related concept to these giving levels is to create a "Club 365," with the idea of giving year-round in exchange for certain perks or benefits. This is an excellent way to encourage consistent annual giving (paid monthly). We've found that many people are drawn to give even more when they will get something in return, and there are definitely donors who like the status of being part of the VIP crowd or one of the "cool kids". They like the exclusivity of being able to access a pre-sale on tickets to an event or a pre-party for the big fundraiser that others don't get to take part in. When creating your Donor Avatar, don't forget to examine touchpoints like this when doing your profiling. Are your A-list donors members at private clubs or do they take part in any VIP activities that you can potentially emulate when designing your own version of the Club 365 program or exclusive VIP donor benefits?

Donor fatigue is a real issue, and it happens when donors are inundated with too many financial requests. Often this happens when nonprofits fail to acknowledge or pay close attention to when and how often a donor is giving. For example, you may have a donor who sends a year end donation as a holiday gift and then in turn receives an ask from your organization in January. Because the calendar year has changed, your nonprofit may be starting a fresh campaign, and—failing to realize that your donor made a very recent contribution—instead of properly acknowledging the recent gift and removing them from this particular round of asks, when the donor receives another right away it creates potential resentment, donor fatigue, likely some frustration for them, and leaves them with the feeling that you're not paying attention and/or valuing their previous donation.

To prevent donor fatigue, you need to follow some simple best practices.

As co-authors, we actually disagree on how often is too often. Michelle believes that at most, you should only be sending one ask per quarter. Darren prefers three per year (an event and two additional asks); they can be much smaller events or smaller campaigns—just pick three and make them all great (with a specific goal in mind for each). Regardless of how many you ultimately choose to do, it's important that each ask is a different *type* of giving (ie. don't invite them to two galas in a calendar year—one is enough).

We have a client that hosts an event of some sort every month. Every two weeks they send an email out to their entire database asking them to support a dance, a bakeshop, a gala, or a concert. They use the same donor list for each ask, and they may have three different email addresses for each individual donor. This is something else to pay close attention to. Many nonprofits are looking to maximize time and are just hitting copy and paste without personalizing their donor communication. You can create donor fatigue even from receiving multiple emails from your organization each time you make an ask, because once again it shows that you aren't paying attention or taking the time to understand your donor's preferences and how they'd like to be contacted. Email is an amazing tool, and adding a small personal detail goes a long way in making your donor feel appreciated and valued.

PRO TIP

If you've invited someone to a ladies' luncheon and they've RSVP'd that they're coming, do not send them anything else asking them to attend that event. Take the time to take them out of the email list for that luncheon so they don't get frustrated when you continue to ask them about an event they have already agreed to attend. Pay attention to who's responding and honor their response by not sending them more stuff!

Target the lists of who you're sending asks and invitations to. Don't send the same thing to everyone in your database every time. This is a common misstep that an organization will make simply because they are strapped for time. They think 'I don't have time to really sort this out and see who came last year and send them a certain targeted email. I'll just send it to everybody and hope it sticks.'

For example, let's say you are planning to have a gala, a ladies' luncheon and an annual campaign. Your donor, Barbara, receives an invitation to all three. Now imagine the surf coach at the high school wants to put on a surf contest as a fundraiser for your organization. You'll want to invest the time to separate and find the group within your database that you would invite specifically to the surf contest. They may be the same type of donors that would be walkers in a walking event, or they might want to cycle in a cycling event. Look for different people than those receiving invitations to the gala and the ladies' luncheon whenever possible. You want to be able to reach out with 3-4 annual asks for different opportunities and events.

While we know this is very time consuming, we promise you that it is absolutely worth it to invest the time necessary to pay very close attention to these types of details and get them right. It's a game changer.

Finally, always avoid the TH-ASK! NEVER include an ask in your thank you or acknowledgement letters or emails! This is not the time nor place to solicit donors—it is ONLY for showcasing your heartfelt gratitude and acknowledgement for their generosity.

WHAT CAN WE OFFER DONORS IN BETWEEN EVENTS?

Since you now know that there is an acceptable maximum for asks in order to avoid donor fatigue, what can you do between events to keep people engaged with your organization? A few of our favorite ideas:

1. Call and invite your donor to a private behind-the-scenes tour of your organization (ie. food bank). This does not involve any financial contribution on the donor's part but

allows them to get involved and offers an opportunity for them to mingle with and meet those they are helping.

2. Send an electronic newsletter quarterly, filled with feel-good stories (and make sure to track the results). This gives you an opportunity to say, "Check out what we are doing because of you and your generosity!"

3. Send a Thanksgiving card that simply says "We're Thankful for YOU."

4. Darren's favorite! Send a thank you 3-6 months after a gala, and include a photo of your donor at the event and share a bit about how their donation has helped your organization. Be sure *not* to include a "Save the Date" for next year's gala; we know how tempting it is to want to save a stamp and make good use of the opportunity by asking for something. But this is just a Thank You. NOTHING ELSE.

5. Donor photos from an event can also be used to highlight your 'hero of the week' or 'donor of the month' on social media. Be sure to tag them if they follow your nonprofit.

BOARD MEMBERS

The question of how to find board members is one we hear often.

First, let's answer this question for start up nonprofits who are figuring out how to build their first board. A great place to start is by asking people who have made a donation to your organization to explore the idea of being a board member and getting on the committee. When somebody has made a donation, especially a larger one, then we know they already believe in the mission. They also have the resources to make a donation of a certain size or more which means they're probably related in some way in terms of friendship or business relationships to others that might be willing to donate. In their circle of influence are other people who could potentially be great donors or board members, so having them represent your board will help to spread your mission.

Remember, no matter the size or stage of life, diversity across your board is imperative. A client recently formed a nonprofit and she asked a group of her friends to be the board members. While they're lovely people, that doesn't necessarily make them the right fit for her board—let alone it being a startup board. She figured out quickly that she needed to diversify, taking it from being a little book club social meeting where they would meet once a month to a meeting focused on events, fundraising, outreach and education. Instead of her group of friends, she needed to bring in specialists who can add value in different ways in areas the organization needs support: an attorney who knows about contracts and governance, and an accountant who can do the books, for example. She realized that if she was reaching out to the right kind of board members there were actually some growing pains she could alleviate or help lessen if she was strategic with people and roles she fulfilled through choosing board members with established expertise that fit with her nonprofit's needs.

Now let's look at intermediate and advanced nonprofits and what you need to focus on when adding new members to an *existing* board. The key is to be strategic here, too—this time in choosing board members who have a diverse and broad circle of influence. For example, what is the outreach capacity of who they are? Perhaps you want a firefighter and a police officer (or both) on your board, because they have a whole community of people that they can bring in to support your fundraising walks. Same thing with people who are high up in the military: they too will have that reach, in addition to a systematic way of thinking and doing things that may prove to be extremely valuable. If your organization is medical, you may want to consider having a doctor on your board who can bring in other doctors and their families and their surgeons to come to your events.

It's important to note that while approaching donors might be a great place to start for new boards, you want to avoid asking your biggest donors and your best volunteers to sit on more established boards. This can create a situation where they become so caught up in the behind the scenes process that they are no longer as motivated to write as large of a check or give additional time to your organization.

MOTIVATING YOUR BOARD TO TAKE ACTION

The best advice we can give is if you want something from your board, you need to ask them for it, and be exact and very specific in your ask.

For example, you need to say, "Ana, I need you to put a table of 10 together for our upcoming event." Be realistic about what you're asking them to do; you want to set them up for success and you want to give them positive reinforcement. You also want to provide whatever tools they need in order to be successful. Follow up your ask to Ana by saying, "We need your table of ten to bring in $5,000. What do you need from me to help you make that happen? Do you need an email invitation? Do you need the sponsorship packet again? Can I send you an email that has exactly what to ask and how to ask for it? How can I help you be successful?" It's important to note that this should be a direct ask in person and not in front of the board because you are likely asking Ana to do something totally different than you would be asking of Jake. Perhaps Jake is a florist in town and he knows the owners of all the other shops on the block. He could probably secure a lot of your in-kind donations by popping in and using his connections to ask those shop owners for a donation versus Ana being able to bring more to the table in financial donations.

Do not just stand in front of the board and say, "Okay everybody, we need tables of 10, we need in-kind donations, and we need sponsorship." What I hear if I'm a volunteer board member when you say this is, "blah blah blah." I'm a board member; I care enough to be here and I do want to help, but I need to be told *exactly* what you want me to do. And then if I say yes, I will commit to it and I'll find a way to get it done. But it can't be a laundry list of things—just one thing. It can be big, but it needs to be focused. You need to ask directly and you need the person to feel supported in the ask so that he or she has the tools to succeed.

VOLUNTEERS

Volunteers are an incredibly important asset to your organization. They give their time and their heart to your mission. You need them in order to be successful in your fundraising efforts. Teach them the mission and they will become active advocates for you. In fact, consider using the 20 second impact statement activity with your volunteers that we described in Chapter 3.

"Before you Recruit Volunteers," an article on volunteer recruitment and retention published by knowhownonprofit.org notes that the traditional route in obtaining volunteers is changing and that organizations are now competing for volunteers. Since volunteers have a growing opportunity to donate their time, many are discriminating about their experience. They want to know that their time is going to be well-spent, the work is well-organized, and that their contribution will be valued.

Volunteers need clear instructions. They want to make sure they know how to carry out their work and that they do it right. You'll want to make the investment into proper volunteer training—for the benefit of both of you. After all, if they do a good job, don't you want them to stick around for the next event? And wouldn't it be wonderful if every time you needed to train someone it was already done—captured in a system and a process that you could deliver to them quickly and without a huge investment of your own time each time? And wouldn't it be amazing if each new volunteer could deliver the results consistently, performing it as well as any seasoned veteran within the organization?

In January 2019, the UK-based National Council for Voluntary Organisations (NCVO) published a report, *Time Well Spent,* on the volunteer experience. This national survey of over 10,000 respondents found there are eight key features that make up a quality experience for volunteers:

1. **Inclusive**: welcome and accessible to all

2. **Flexible**: takes into account people's individual life circumstances

3. **Impactful**: makes a positive difference

4. **Connected**: gives a sense of connection to others, to the cause and/or an organization

5. **Balanced**: does not over-burden with unnecessary processes

6. **Enjoyable**: provides enjoyment, people feel good about what they are doing

7. **Voluntary**: the volunteer has freely chosen to do it

8. **Meaningful**: resonates with volunteers' lives, interests and priorities

SOURCING VOLUNTEERS

Volunteer programs have long been an integrated part of large corporations and can be an excellent source for volunteers. Kohl's, for instance, has a volunteer program and in 2018 alone, their associates contributed more than 300,000 volunteer hours.

Social responsibility continues to increase as a focus among corporations. According to Thomas Bognanno, corporate social responsibility has evolved dramatically over the last decade. Most companies are no longer satisfied with just writing checks to charities or sponsoring events. Now, corporate leaders are aligning social impact and employee engagement with business objectives. That means measuring results and ensuring corporate social responsibility and employee engagement efforts demonstrate real value to the company.

Another fantastic idea for sourcing volunteers is to approach a neighboring nonprofit and offer to share your well-versed volunteers. For example, if you are both hosting galas, offer to send your board to go volunteer at their event to do check in. They know the system, they know the routine, and they know the process which is an enormous asset. There is a time advantage as well, when Edwin or Jane walks up to check in, the volunteers won't know them so it goes a lot faster. When you have your own board at the table for check in, the amount of time required to greet and exchange pleasantries with each attendee can slow the check in process to a crawl. So team up with another nonprofit where you can switch volunteer crews, you work their event and they work yours. This is our favorite recommendation for having trained event volunteers for no cost.

FINDING YOUR TEAMS

Unless you are a brand new organization, you probably have people who have volunteered in the past. The Event Chair should reach out to them well in advance of the event to determine whether or not they want to be involved again as a team leader or volunteer. Host a volunteer recruiting party with wine and cheese, make it a fun night out.

If you still need volunteers, consider asking people who know and understand the cause, even if they've never volunteered before. Former donors who may have given smaller amounts previously, but also give regularly, can be perfect volunteers. They have proven they are interested and loyal to your cause and often enjoy the opportunity to play a more active role in your organization's success. However, as we mentioned earlier in the book, avoid asking your larger donors to be volunteers. We want their focus to remain on being a financial supporter. If you are an organization that serves people directly, your own clients or their families are often willing to help. These volunteers usually show their passion for your organization and end up being wonderful volunteers and ambassadors, as they have seen first hand all the good it does!

After exhausting all of your internal sources, if you find that you still need some extra hands, contact local service organizations such as Rotary, Jr League, Civitan, Kiwanis, Elks and even retail chains. Have staff members go through their contact lists and ask board members to do the same. Think about contacts through the Chambers of Commerce and young professionals networking groups. Often young professionals don't have the money to attend all the galas, but will work at them as a volunteer. This also helps build a base of future board members and donors as they progress through their careers!

Build a Winning Team

The date has been confirmed, the theme chosen, and it is time to start working on the event. As with any important occasion, you want to gather the very best people to support the cause. The more committed and informed your "A" team is, the more you can ensure a successful event.

The word *"committee"* however, probably makes the hairs on the back of your neck stand up. We've all sat through plenty of unproductive committee meetings! However, committees, or *"teams"* as we like to call them, are essential to the success of an event. You are only one person and you need many others involved to accomplish your goals.

But, what if you're a small nonprofit with only a few staff members? You may think it is impossible to assemble an event committee when your staff, after all, is busy attending to the day-to-day operations of the organization. While this thought process is logical, it is also disastrous. You may believe that there is no way—or time—to successfully run an event committee while at the same time effectively operating the business of your nonprofit—but you must find a way. Any great endeavor requires planning and ingenuity. It is a large undertaking, unquestionably, yet with some creative thinking it's definitely something you can accomplish. Let me illustrate with a real-life example from my own career.

I had just accepted an opportunity as Development Officer with a National nonprofit and I couldn't wait to join the team. Walking into the door of my new office, I was both elated and nervous to meet the staff and my fellow colleagues. In my initial meeting with them that afternoon, we reviewed the calendar of events when someone mentioned the upcoming benefit gala.

"Great!" I said, enthusiastic about hitting the ground running. "Who is on the committee for the gala? I see it's only three months away."

The two staff members looked at each other and started laughing. One said, "We don't have volunteer committees in this office." The other one said, "our people don't like the C-word."

When I recently told this story to the new executive director who just started last week, she asked me, "So, what did you do?"

I responded, "I created a committee called 'Team Gala'." I started by asking questions about last year's gala:

- Was there an honoree or special guest spotlighted at the event?
- Who was the number one fundraising sponsor?
- Was there a guest speaker or an active volunteer?

My new colleagues were able to point me to all these key individuals. I reached out to each of them, had coffee with them, and asked what they loved about last year's gala as well as what they thought needed to be different this year.

I always suggest sending surveys after events in order to gather valuable information from attendees, volunteers and sponsors, but this is something different. This is a one-to-one ask in an advisory role where you are looking not just for their opinion, but to the level of expertise they bring from attending many events for your organization. Often, attendees and donors will have been in an organization much longer than a staff member, development officer, or even an executive director. So you can give them the role of "event veteran" and not only learn a lot from what they tell you, but enlist their support as a volunteer or donor.

Overall, the results of reaching out to all these key individuals were amazing and returned a multitude of rewards. We received some valuable feedback on how to make the event better, deepened our engagement with those already committed to our cause, and gained some new members to "Team Gala." All it took was reaching out to a few individuals who were deeply vested in our cause. It can be easy to fall into the trap of having to do it all yourself. Look around, there may be more resources than you think.

If you are able to call a larger group together from your volunteer and sponsor base, ideally your "Team Gala" should be comprised of the following committee roles:

- Event Chair(s)/Co-Chair(s)
- Media Lead
- Honoree and/or Guest Speaker (more about this below)
- Procurement Queen/King
- Volunteer Coordinator
- Sponsorship Guru
- Décor Lead
- Vendor Liaison
- Program Author/Editor (for scripts, speeches and acknowledgements)

Each of the above individuals may lead a subcommittee, which may or may not include other members of the team, and chooses the role they would like. Note we use the term "choose" lightly here.

CREATING YOUR TEAMS

In the best-selling book, *You Win in the Locker Room First: The Seven "Cs" of a Winning Team in Business, Sports, and Life,* former head coach of the Atlanta Falcons, Mike Smith, and Jon Gordon, consultant to many college and professional sports teams, discuss seven principles that any team can apply to get on top of their game. The Seven C's of any winning team, including a fundraising team, are: Culture, Contagious (as in energy), Consistency, Communication, Connect(ion), Commitment, and Caring. Your fundraising results will be served well if you build a team embodying these key characteristics.

One of the Cs of a winning team is Connection, and you can best create a feeling of connectedness for your committee members to your cause by ensuring they are engaged in roles and activities they enjoy. When assembling a committee, keep the following objectives in mind in order to optimize each committee member's experience:

- Determine what a committee member might "love" to do. If one of your committee members owns a car dealership, he or she would likely be good at vendor contract negotiations. If you have a florist on the committee, or someone says, "my best friend is a florist,"—Bingo—Décor! Volunteers themselves are usually great at recognizing where they will be comfortable, so listen to them. The last thing you want is a bunch of angry volunteers who aren't getting to do what they love. For example, CPA's are great at data entry, and the check-in/out position. Outgoing members or high level donors can make great greeters or table captains. A volunteer who is a real people-person would likely not be your best fit for a behind the scenes role like decorations. People with sales experience can be valuable at the live auction display and silent auction tables, drawing interest to the items, engaging with the attendees etc. Well-organized folk who are a little more shy may be great at item pick-up, decorations, or logistics. Therefore, taking the time to understand each person's interests, strengths, and challenges will be important to ensuring everyone is given the right position for their talent and interest.

- Have a specific role for each member, with tasks for each that have measurable goals and timelines. These are not assigned goals, they are developed by and with the committee.

The best experience for committee members is when the meetings are planned (standard day and time), organized (send the agenda the day before and ask for feedback) and start and end on time (a challenge but so important).

HONOREES AND GUEST SPEAKERS

If your event has someone who will be honored or will serve as a guest speaker, consider including them on the volunteer planning committee. Here is why:

They know the cause.

If you have chosen someone to honor because they are a

generous donor, volunteer or are associated with a direct beneficiary of your non-profit and therefore serving as a guest speaker, they are well versed in the "language" your organization speaks. The honoree will not only bring their friends, family and fans as guests, but by participating in the planning will naturally adopt a sense of ownership for the event. This can lead to new sponsorship opportunities, active auction item procurement efforts, and the recruitment of close friends to join the committee.

Note: The honoree should not be the event chair or co-chair, if possible. The more members on the committee, the more guests in the room—period. I can hear some of you saying, "Too many chefs spoil the pot." While that can be true, if you, as a leader of the team can manage the committee and supporting sub-committees, then the more the merrier.

Once you have your team, take the time to train them. This will help foster a Culture (another C of a winning team) of superior customer service with your volunteers. As a united team you can create an unforgettable event that is both rewarding and financially successful. Provide volunteers enough information for them to feel empowered in solving issues on the spot. Provide cheat sheets and committee/ team captain names for the volunteers to communicate issues or problems as they arise. True "event people" know, that events require thinking on your feet. Unforeseen problems can occur without warning. Knowing who has the power to make a quick decision will make the event run seamlessly, where only the committee is aware of anything that didn't follow the script.

Committee meetings should be held in a professional setting (nonprofit offices or conference rooms as available). This will lead to more professional demeanor and accountability. Save the happy hour for the post-event celebration. Have snacks and drinks available (or better yet, pre-assigned) for meetings. Be realistic with expectations regarding meeting length, stick to the agenda, and work to accommodate the majority of the team members' schedules, knowing that you won't be able to please everyone. Additionally, running the meetings in a relaxed, happy—yet professional manner will allow volunteers to feel safe in the group to share their thoughts, at the same time building trust and camaraderie with fellow teammates. Differences of opinions on committees is to be expected, yet can be tremendously productive, if handled with care. The team's success counts on it. Each of us knows that the challenges we face and overcome together make us a stronger, close-knit team that can do amazing things.

Poor planning leads to stress, stress, and more stress. Under pressure, important details fall through the cracks. This is neither the time nor place to try to do everything yourself. In fact, this sort of thinking actually sets your event up for failure. So take the time to choose a team you know you can count on—a team that is passionate, responsible, and will get the job done.

Ideally, you should develop three separate committees for each event:

1. Planning Committee
2. Event Committee
3. Stewardship Committee

Now that we have each committee, following are the key team players along with a definition of each role. Keep in mind, it is a good idea to include a job description for each of the team leaders you choose. Having a job description not only helps with recruitment, it sets clear expectations right off the bat for that specific role.

The Event Chair/Co-chair

The event Chair/Co-chair is a volunteer position and is generally selected by a member of your staff, likely the Development Officer. The Chair may be a board member or even a beneficiary, and you are looking for someone who knows the cause and is committed to it, has excellent interpersonal skills, is very organized, and can communicate clearly. Additionally, it is important this person really has the time to devote to this event. They are the Committee Lead, responsible for the nuts and bolts of the event from the nonprofits perspective. The event Chair/Co-chair will oversee all other team leaders and also interact with potential donors, board members, volunteers, sponsors, attendees, and vendors, so choose wisely.

The Media Lead

This person will be responsible for working with your webmaster to create the event page; update your social media as the event gets closer (or work with your social media professional); get your event on local calendars; oversee the printing of flyers, save-the-date announcements, programs, invitations, and thank you cards. Additionally, this person will manage press releases for your event. Because of all of this, be sure to consider this person carefully, as they are responsible for your brand and image on social media. In short, this person needs to be very socially connected and have a deep understanding of your organization's brand and identity. They

MUST value and respect the role, in one email or phone call they can upset a relationship.

Procurement Queen/King

The Auction Team Leader will oversee both the live and silent auction teams. This is a very big job and requires someone with good contacts in the community and the ability to procure auction items and/or the ability to manage people effectively that do have the ability to procure said items. This person should be mission driven. They need to think carefully about the type of items that donors and guests will find interesting and they should be looking for experiences, opportunities that guests can't simply find and buy online. When asking companies to donate, most people will simply ask the company in question to donate items, and never really give them a reason why they are asking for that specific item or explaining how that specific donation will make a difference to their non-profit organization. This can then lead to fewer donations and a lack of enthusiasm from your donors, which you want to avoid. Your Lead should be sure to share when asking that the gift or donation could help raise $1500 which would send nine kids to camp or fund a day of research. Make it real for them and show them how much they will truly be helping.

The auction teams will ultimately procure, organize, package, enter, deliver, and set-up the items for the live and silent auctions. This will include obtaining consignment items if you use them; locating storage for preparation of bid items; preparing bid sheets or mobile bidding platforms; staging the silent auction; and creating the slideshow and displays for the live auction items. Furthermore, at the end of the event, the Auction Team will facilitate delivery of auction items to winning bidders.

Volunteer Coordinator

This vitally important person will determine the number of volunteers needed and they will be responsible to recruit, train, and manage them during the actual event. Additionally, they will be in charge of taking care of these volunteers and their needs, including finding a way to provide food/water for them the day of the event.

Sponsorship Guru

Without sponsors and underwriters, events are not financially successful. This team will be responsible, along with the fund development team, board members, and Executive Director, for obtaining event sponsors and underwriters. They will also manage the design and printing of sponsor/underwriter banners, posters, table recognition or other mutually agreed-upon recognition.

Check-in/Check-out Leader

This team leader will design and implement check-in and check-out procedures for the beginning and end of the event. They will deal with the money handling procedures, the collection of funds, and the distribution of receipts and oversee the event software for the evening— if it is used. They will work with the Volunteer Coordinator to ensure each reception volunteer is trained appropriately, procure and organize the bidder numbers, manage guest registrations both before and at the event, and maintain the guest database through the end of the event. They will coordinate the check-out and distribution of Live and Silent auction items.

Vendor Liaison

The Vendor Liaison will oversee all of the working parts behind the scenes: valet parking, directional signage, coat check, direction for volunteers, registration table location, bars and liquor, easels, podium and microphone, sound system, screens and projectors, temperature and ventilation, trash cans, etc. In short, they will be working directly with each team leader, helping them set up, directing the space, and making sure the event room itself is set up in such a way that makes sense and gives everyone convenient access to what it is they need.

Décor Lead

This is the team with flair. The leader of this team will work to oversee the coordination of the theme of your event, really helping to bring it to life. From table centerpieces, to cutlery, to menu choices, to specialty drinks, this team leader's focus will be in making sure everyone has a great time in a beautiful setting. Additionally, this team leader and the team will arrive early the day of the event and set up the tables, decorations, put up the donor posters, arrange centerpieces, help arrange the silent auction displays, ensure that the entertainment arrives and gets through their sound check, and takes care of all the details that make for a great experience.

Program Lead

This lead takes ownership of the event day timeline, run of show, slides/video production and program book. Working with the event planner from the venue, the speakers and auctioneer/MC, the entertainment, and the AV team to create a memorable experience for your guests.

Table Captain

There should be a table captain for each table you have at your event. This role is not officially part of the event committee, but it is an important element in the fundraising equation. Each Table Captain will be responsible for filling his or her table with guests who have the ability and financial means. It is important that Table Captains know they shouldn't just fill their tables with office staff or family that may not financially support the cause. They need to bring people who will actively participate in the event and give to the cause. Table Captains will often be invited guests, but don't always have to be.

Each of these leaders may have a large number of team members working with them to accomplish the tasks assigned to them. By assigning team leaders and having regular team meetings with the event captain, you can ensure each team is progressing as well as keep the communication flowing. Limiting the number of team leaders to less than ten also improves the effectiveness of team meetings.

SPONSORS

Sponsors and underwriters are people who will give money or products to your organization to specifically defray the cost of your event (though they may wish to donate funds to your charity as well). In return for this, sponsors and underwriters will generally receive some sort of advertising and marketing at your event, and depending upon the level of giving, prior to the event. Fiscal vibrancy of any charitable organization depends on its ability to find, nurture, and maintain sponsors. This endeavor however, is a blend of art and science and requires your entire team to work closely together. Staff, volunteers, and board members all have an important role to play in building your supporting cast.

In the event world, we classify sponsors and underwriters differently. Sponsors pay large sums of money either for recognition, family/personal legacy, marketing benefits or adhere to corporate giving programs. Underwriters usually underwrite with minimum to no revenue profit from the underwriting. This can also be an "in-kind" sponsor who provide sprinting free, for example, or at a discount.

KNOW YOUR IDENTITY AND PURPOSE

This could be a fun team-building exercise where you do two things: Revisit and refresh your vision and mission, and examine and establish your organizational goals. Sponsors want to know what you are about and if their vision and mission are a good match for yours. Having a clearly-defined mission statement and well-developed organizational goals, that your team has helped to develop, engages your sponsor team in the process.

Spend some time delving into the demographics of your clientele, audience members, and potential donors. Potential sponsors will want to know if your target event audience is a fit for their product. For example, if your organization is an elementary school foundation, it is probable that both your clientele and event audience are mostly school parents between the ages of 25-35, so grocery stores, school and office supply stores, big box stores, even the local Apple store, might be good sponsors to consider.

If your organization is a dog rescue, your event audience will be dog-lovers. Pet food companies, pet stores, veterinarians, and groomers might be a good fit. If you run a youth organization, however, it is possible that your clientele and event audience are widely different and thus could appeal to a much broader range of sponsors.

FINDING THE RIGHT SPONSORS

Finding the right sponsors can provide long-term funding for your organization and save you time in the long-run. It is easy to get caught up in the hamster wheel of calling everybody you've ever come in contact with to see if they'd like to be a sponsor. It is far more effective to consider sponsorship as a role that needs to be cast and you are looking for the perfect actor to own that particular role. The sponsors, on the other hand, are looking for the perfect match "role" that will further their career, organization's philanthropic mission, or enhance their business.

Start your "casting search" by making a list of businesses—local, regional and national, that are related to your cause. Assign research to one or more of your team that are techie web searchers.

For example, if your charity provides resources to women with breast cancer and their families, identify businesses in the area that might be a good fit. In this instance, you have four main groups: businesses that cater to the medical industry; businesses that provide services to families that are going through this struggle, such as daycare centers and food services; businesses that cater to therapy and emotional support; and business that may not be directly related to the issue but have made massive efforts to help better the lives of those who suffer via research-funding and support. In this instance, the local daycare or a local therapy practice might be a fantastic sponsor, as well as a national business like Yoplait —a company well known for its donations to fund research to cure breast cancer.

Ancillary sponsor potential: Every community has "good corporate citizens" who regularly support causes within the community. This is often found on their websites or local Chambers of Commerce.

Many businesses that are just entering the local marketplace will also be looking for ways to make an impact in the local community. However, you are not alone in reaching out to these businesses. Thousands of NPOs are doing the same thing. Sending letters and emails is the easy route, instead, pick up the phone and make the calls, a personal ask goes a long way.

Once you've created your list, sit down and brainstorm with the full sponsorship team as well as the Board of Directors to see who might have contacts to your target prospects. Prioritize the order in which potential sponsors will be contacted and by whom. If no contact exists, reach out to those in your circle of influence to find possible connections to the businesses. Some fund developers have even begun to use social media to reach out and find connections to businesses and corporations by posting requests for contact people. Before you approach a business, however, be sure to do your research into that particular business's rules and regulations surrounding sponsorships and philanthropy. You don't want to walk into an organization and ask for sponsorship, only to have the manager direct you to their online website.

MAKING YOUR SPONSORS FEEL SPECIAL

Each sponsor, no matter how large or how small, wants to feel that they have a valuable part to play in your production. Some will have a much larger role than others, however, all are needed for your fundraising event to be fully realized. With competition for sponsorship dollars increasing due to the rising number of charitable organizations, the need to bring value to a sponsor's role is magnified. Simply having a contact is not enough anymore.

Gone are the days of simply placing their logo on a table, thanking them at the event, and giving them a table of seat-fillers. Sponsors today are looking for ways to have active, engaging roles, not just a cameo appearance. Today's sponsor wants unique opportunities that provide brand equity and a relationship with your cause. Some want to be the hero, while others want to see their impact in the overall fundraising strategy. Give them plenty of reasons to choose you.

CREATING A UNIQUE ROLE: SPONSOR BENEFITS

You have a unique opportunity in today's world to offer a wide variety of sponsor benefits. It is possible that each sponsor over a certain dollar amount would have a completely customized sponsorship package. Sponsor "A" might want to have a live link in each newsletter because they are most interested in reaching your clientele. Sponsor "B" might prefer branding opportunities like placement of their logo behind the event selfie station or step and repeat wall, thereby increasing their social media reach and impressions. Other opportunities could include a sponsor-provided informational seminar for your clients and donors, brand recognition on your printed materials, or video interviews on the event website. The sponsorship offerings are truly up to you. However, it can be helpful when you are dealing with a potentially game-changing sponsor, to think of them as a star actor. Be willing to create a role that will make them happy, feel fully appreciated, and exhibit respect for what they bring to the organization.

Your sponsor team will need to work with your board to decide at what levels you are willing to negotiate benefits. Perhaps sponsors below the $5,000/year level receive a prescribed benefit package, but sponsors above that level receive a personalized package. That is entirely up to your team, but note that personalization does take time.

PLACING THEM ON CENTER STAGE: PROMOTING YOUR SPONSOR'S BRAND

Sponsors ultimately engage in charitable giving to promote their service, product, and brand. Sponsor activation refers to the manner in which you engage the sponsors' brands. Traditional methods, mentioned earlier, involve table logos, banners, and an advertisement in a program. As our world becomes increasingly digital, mobile and global, savvy sponsors ask for new ways to be an active sponsor and to increase their impact per sponsor dollar.

Increase the value to your sponsors at the event by providing them an opportunity to have an interactive booth or to provide giveaways to guests. This opens the communication channel between your event attendees and your all-star sponsors.

For example, a local bakery wanted to sponsor an event for a youth organization. Instead of giving a cash donation, however, they provided a cake for every table, each of which were auctioned off at the end of the night. Not only did this cake company get extra air time during the auction, many tables also cut into their cakes to share together before they left, thus allowing everyone to sample the cake company's goods.

Additionally, the use of social media, websites, e-newsletters, and mobile platforms can elevate an event sponsorship by engaging potentially thousands of people who do not even attend the event.

REAL LIFE EXAMPLE

In the example given earlier with the selfie booth, guests were given the opportunity during the cocktail hour to step into the "selfie booth" and take a picture. A step and repeat wall that repeated the sponsor's logo alongside the organization's logo, served as the backdrop (think Oscars). Guests were asked to post it on social media with a hashtag of both the charity and the sponsor. 100 selfies posted on social media turned into 10,000 views of the sponsors logo.

MAINTAINING YOUR SPONSORS OVER TIME (SPONSOR STEWARDSHIP)

Thanking them personally and in writing is, of course, required. However, to truly build the relationship, it is important to talk with your sponsors about their experience and future expectations.

After the event is over, discuss their satisfaction with their branding and visibility. What did they like? What do they think could have been done better? Discuss ways to improve in future events. Ensure they understand that this is indeed a partnership, and you want them to be satisfied with the value of their sponsorship. This simple step will put your organization ahead of many who do not understand the value of developing a relationship based on mutual benefit. In other words, this is the first step in developing a sponsor into a funder. Funders provide support in the form of funding, time commitment, and assistance all year long, making them a funder versus a one-time donor.

VENDORS

Behind every great event is a crew of hardworking, dedicated professionals and volunteers whose work goes largely under appreciated. The guests may see and interact with a handful of staff and volunteers, the Executive Director, the auctioneer, and some board members. However, most of them have no idea about the number of people needed to make the vision of the event they are experiencing become a reality. Choosing the correct third-party vendors (such as catering, event planners, auctioneers and entertainment), and developing a relationship with each of them can have a significant impact on the success of your event.

The Event Planner is the most critical job on the vendor list. Because of this, a paid professional should almost always be considered for this role. While the initial cost may be a bit frightening, event planners can be worth their weight in gold. This is because the amount of effort it takes to successfully pull off an event like this is significant. If you try to plan the event yourself, you will likely be unable to successfully run your organization as well. Simply put, there is no way you can have a full time position in your organization and act as the event planner as well. If you try, you are setting yourself up for some serious stress, lack of sleep, and needless mishaps. Additionally, paid event planners have access to resources and lists that you won't have. They have great contacts with bands, auctioneers, caterers etc. We'll discuss Event Planners in more detail, including how to pick the right one, in the second half of the book.

There are a couple of important considerations regarding third party vendors.

First, there is a fee for free. We all secretly (or openly) dream that all of our vendors will provide their services as a donation. After all, it is an amazing cause! Unfortunately, this rarely happens. It is always tempting to use vendors who are friends or relatives of employees or board members. Let me offer a word of caution based upon experience. Take a moment and consider the motivations for hiring friends and relatives. While the services these people provide may be free, remember, the success of the event is contingent upon the experience, equipment quality, and professionalism provided to your guests. If the motivation for hiring a specific vendor is a relationship to someone in the organization which can provide discounted prices, this may not be the vendor relationship that provides the most benefit to the cause.

Do your best to view all proposed vendors through the same lens. Who will be the best partner for the organization over time? Does this person or company have good reviews and a good reputation in the business community? Food delivered cold or flowers that arrive wilted can really have a detrimental effect on your event, so be sure to vet every vendor—regardless of relationship, and your fundraising will reflect your dedication in the long run.

Remember, vendors are not invited guests. They should not participate in the party unless invited by a staff member in advance to celebrate and they certainly should not be drinking during the event.

CHAPTER 7
GOING DIGITAL - THE IMPORTANCE OF TECHNOLOGY IN FUNDRAISING

We've already briefly discussed how the internet has worked to drastically change the face of fundraising. However, mobile platforms have certainly played their part in this technological advancement as well. For example, donors can now access information about your organization, verify your credibility, and donate online all within a matter of minutes.

This is important because apart from allowing you to gather more funds than ever before, younger donors in particular are becoming increasingly critical about organizations, expecting to have information easily available to them both before and after they give. Therefore, distinct differences in giving trends between younger and older donors will require organizations to stay current (having information readily available through the internet and various mobile platforms) or risk losing a whole new generation of donors.

Because of this, we thought it would be prudent to discuss some of the most important technological tools available to organizations today and how they can affect your bottom line.

Before getting into specifics, however, it is important to note that you need to investigate a few things before taking the plunge with any type of software or technological tool. For example, you need to know how many users are allowed, what kind of technical support is provided—and at what cost, and with what other programs and features it integrates easily. If you find the answers to these questions meet your needs and expectations, then by all means consider using them. However, some of these programs and tools do have hidden fees and regulations, so make sure you do all of your research beforehand so you can be sure to find the right options for you.

CUSTOMER AND CLIENT RELATIONSHIP MANAGEMENT SOFTWARE

Customer Relationship Management Software (or CRMs) is software businesses use to keep track of their customers, allowing them to send promotions, personalized thank you's and even see the last time said customer purchased something. Because of this, CRMs have been a staple in the business world for many years.

That said, CRMs are not just for for-profit businesses. They are essential in the nonprofit world as well, because as with a for-profit business, your customers are your life. Without accurate information about them, you cannot cultivate and maintain a healthy business relationship. It doesn't matter that you aren't in the business of creating a profit for yourself, you are in business; you are working to raise money for your cause. Therefore, your most important assets are those individuals and businesses that fund your cause.

How will it benefit your organization exactly to use a CRMs? For starters, it will greatly increase your donor communication and tracking. For example, a good nonprofit will follow up with even the smallest of their donors, sending personalized thank you's to everyone, thus making them feel special and appreciated. As a nonprofit, your goal is to be a great steward for your donors, ensuring they know their donations not only help the cause but are greatly appreciated, thus cultivating a giving relationship that will last for years to come. CRMS therefore, are essential because they allow you to keep track of everyone, ensuring nobody slips through the cracks and nobody is ever forgotten.

Donor communication aside, CRMs can also help you track your volunteer hours for grants and annual reports, not to mention streamline data entry. For instance, rather than inputting donor and volunteer contact information and history into multiple systems, it can be entered once, saving personnel expenses as well as reducing human error.

CRMs are a great tool for grouping your donors, volunteers and sponsors so that it is quick and simple to select a crowd for a particular event or ask. They offer customized fields and attributes that you can make specific to the makeup of your organization. If, for example, you are in the education field, your personalized attributes list might include the option to select a parent, a teacher or a school employee. Are they a first time donor? Are they on the board? Are they a former board member? Are they an alumni? The aim is to develop a list of attributes that will allow you to target the right audience for your organization. In a previous chapter we referenced Giving Circles, and your custom CRMS software fields are the perfect place to designate those giving levels.

EVENT MANAGEMENT SOFTWARE

Event Management Software (EMS) is a remarkable tool that can facilitate a much more positive experience for your guests and yield higher revenue for your charity. It is essential to the success of any sort of fundraising event your organization might endeavor to take on, because it provides an easy way to handle all aspects of an event and to produce very helpful data afterwards. This is hugely important in determining not only what your next event will be, as well as where it will be, who you will invite, etc, but also helpful in creating your budget and projections for the next year via statistics and contacts. Basically, event software will provide for a much more organized event once all of the input has been done upfront.

There are many Event Management Software programs currently on the market for you to choose from, such as *Greater Giving*, *Bid Pal*, and *Silent Auction Pro* that provide a wide variety of features to fit your organization's every need.

Here are a few important considerations to make when choosing software:

- Does the software company provide the hardware (computers and printers) if you do not have them?

- What training do they provide?

- Do you have a direct contact person?

- What levels of customer support do they provide?

- What types of reports can you run?

- What are the features of their packages and what are the fees for each?

- Do they provide demonstration models for you to use?

- How many volunteers or staff members will it take to run the software?

- Do they provide the manpower if you don't have enough?

- Do they provide on-site staff for support?

MOBILE BIDDING PLATFORMS

Mobile bidding is the hot new trend in silent auctions. Featuring the ability to bid on items via texting and/or smartphone apps, these platforms bring auctions into the 21st century. Furthermore, research shows if you utilize mobile bidding effectively, you have the potential to raise your organization's income by up to 30%, which is a huge benefit when competition for donor dollars is at an all time high.

Things to consider Before Choosing a Bidding Platform For Your Event

This is certainly an exciting statistic and a great reason to get excited about hopping on the mobile bidding platform train. Before leaping in, however, there are some things you absolutely need to consider.

First, you need to evaluate your guests' technological capabilities. If your guests are not avid smartphone or tablet users, for example, using a mobile bidding platform could be a disastrous endeavor. As we've already discussed, you want to make it as easy as possible for your donors to give. You don't want it to be a chore for them because if it is, you will lose money.

Second, you need to evaluate your own technological capabilities. If, for example, your venue does not have the infrastructure to handle a huge influx of people accessing Wifi at once, it could bring your auction to a screeching halt. This is because either the Wifi could crash all together, or the network itself could begin running extremely slow. Think of it like rush hour. When everyone tries to get onto the highway at the same time, it causes back ups and slow downs because there simply isn't enough room for everyone to enter and use the highway at once. The internet works much the same way. There's a single digital "door" and even if it is fairly large, if you have 750 people trying to squeeze through this door all at once, it isn't going to work. This then will lead to a major loss of funds as well as frustrated donors. That is a major lose-lose.

Therefore, if you do choose to go with a mobile bidding platform, you need to spare no expense when it comes to your Wifi connection. Again, you want to make it as easy as possible for your donors to give you money, and if they experience extended delays in being able to bid, they will lose interest, especially in this age of instant gratification. Mobile bidding platforms may not be recommended for events where there will be under 500 people in attendance and should never be used for a live auction, due to the fact it is not fast paced enough (even with the best Wifi available), and can take away greatly from the energy and excitement a live auction thrives on.

Benefits to a Mobile Bidding Platform

If you do decide that a mobile bidding platform is right for your event and organization, there are many benefits that come with its use:

- Guests can pre-register.

- Guests are notified when they have been outbid, thus promoting increased bidding.

- Bidders don't have to attend the event itself to participate, thereby widening your audience significantly.

- Guests can bid from anywhere in the room so they don't have to fight the crowds or leave a conversation just to bid.

- Guests can set maximum bid alerts and be alerted via text message.

- Gives a modern and cutting edge feel to your event.

- Can excite bidders!

- Can save you time if you link it with your event software, because you don't need to input winners.

- Allows bidding to continue after the event or take place beforehand with online auctions for special items. This provides more people the opportunity to participate and can increase your revenue

EVENTOLOGY 101
THE DNA OF A FUNDRAISING EVENT

PLANNING · EVENT · STEWARDSHIP

CHAPTER 8
GUEST FOCUSED EVENT MANAGEMENT

The guest experience IS everything. The guests are at the center of every decision and every action as you prepare for the next over-the-top event. Fundraising is an experience, make it memorable.

UNDERSTANDING STEWARDSHIP

Even though stewardship comes last, it really comes first. While many see stewardship as the nonprofit's relationship with a donor after they have contributed to the organization, it truly starts with us building the relationship with the donor first and foremost. When we can come to learn the donor's preferences and vision for their contributions to our cause, we can better respond to their needs. This is no different when it comes to event fundraising, specifically.

A guest-focused event experience is the way to maximize the return on your event investment.

There are many components in organizing and executing a successful event. The event flow is critically important, and therefore, you will want to give each piece considerable thought and attention. Every detail makes a difference ... and EVERYTHING is tied to fundraising.

Just imagine, it's your big night, it's cold outside, no one told you when you booked the venue that they had a wedding on the other side of the property. Your donors are waiting in a long valet line to leave the car, and when they get out of the car, the staff doesn't even know where to direct them. Your guests are getting upset before they even find your event room.

As they approach check in, how long is the line? Is anyone serving drinks while the guest are waiting to check in? Are board members working the line and greeting the guests, thanking them for coming? Again, every detail matters.

WHO - WHAT - HOW

You and your team have the same goal. You want to create an experience for your guests that will linger in their minds and hearts long after the event ends. You want them to leave your event excited about every donation dollar they contributed to your cause. More importantly, you want your guests feeling valued enough that they'll donate again. This starts with your detailed plan. You've heard the saying, "The devil is in the details." An event may seem effortless at first, but will take more time and work than expected. Start planning the day following the last event.

You must set the foundation for your event by determining your specific goals. Making this event unforgettable is a huge undertaking, you need to get creative and be ready to stand out.

- Who is your audience – demographics and capacity to give?

- What would deem your event a success? Net profit is key. Do the math.

- What theme will the event carry from promotion to conclusion?

- How do you follow up post-event?

THE WHY (THE GOAL/MISSION)

The purpose of your event cannot be overstated, and its messaging should move all those involved at every level from problem to solution; to join you in the journey of solving this problem through your mission. That's why before you can dive into the details of an event plan, you must know why you are holding the event. In considering the purpose for the event and your audience, you must answer these questions:

- Why are we having this event? (Fund-raiser vs. Friend-raiser)

- Which guest do we (not) want to attend this event?

- How do we want the guests to feel when they leave?

Some groups host events to primarily educate potential donors about the cause and hope to raise a bit of money in the process. Others simply want their members to spend some time together having a good time to show their appreciation and create bonds, often referred to as a "friend-raiser". Alternately, some organizations will host an event that is focused solely on the fundraising - where it's all about the money. Knowing the type of event you want to create will determine how you plan everything from where the event will be held, to who will be invited.

If, for example, the event's main purpose is to educate people or for people to enjoy themselves, thus bringing in potential new donors, a midweek luncheon at a board member's house or local restaurant would be an appropriate event. In this more intimate setting, people are invited as personal guests, are more relaxed, and more thoughtful, therefore leading to more intentional conversations. If, however, this is primarily a fundraising event for your organization, then it must be designed with that pure intent. The timeline for the event, setup of the room, and sound system (no using a bullhorn) will need to be focused on how to raise the most funds possible for your organization.

How can you set yourself apart from the three competing events in the city that night? What can you offer that draws a guest, donor or sponsor to your event? After you've decided the type of event, get to know your potential audience. What are their habits, passions, pastimes, work relationships, and common goals? Do they want to leave a legacy? Are they passionate about a cause because of a family member or personal experience? Knowing the audience will further assist you in creating the right experience for them. As you learn more about them you will also have the benefit of building a personal relationship. In a perfect world, the connections you make through preparation make the decision easy for the guest to decide to attend your event.

DETERMINING THE EVENT TYPE

Events of any kind can be one of the most impactful ways to connect with supporters of your cause. An intimate cocktail reception, luncheon or even a breakfast can be a great fundraiser. Host a corn hole tournament, pickle ball challenge, or a bowl-a-thon to bring a new twist to the smaller type of fundraising. Think about the size of your audience and the financial goal. Thinking about a Gala? Are you ready to do all the work to plan and host? More importantly, are you ready for the follow up and reach out to each guest after the event? This follow up is 100% a MUST in consideration of next year's gala. The real work really kicks in the week after the gala/event and goes on for another 365 days till the next event :)

WHEN

In most traditional markets, March, April, May and Late August, September, October and November are the BIG fundraising months. Friday and Saturday are the easy go-to dates. That limits your fundraising opportunities significantly; with only 28 weekends.

A challenge you may face will be competition for your donor's time. How many other amazing nonprofits are going to have events on the top 28 weekends? There are often hundreds and in some markets, thousands of competing events. With weddings, graduations, and holidays all competing for your donor's personal time, we suggest that you consider a Tuesday or Thursday. Oftentime venues and event vendors are excited to book midweek events, as these are generally slower days for venues, you may even get a break on the price. Additionally, you are not frequently running into the conflict of weddings at venues during the week, and the event you host may be a bit more condensed, with a shorter timeline, making for a greater impact.

SELECTING A THEME

A theme sets the tone, décor, food, entertainment and promotion for the entire event. Consider your desired audience before choosing the theme. The theme that you select for your event should be congruent with your audience, purpose, and message. For instance, a Brew Fest is most likely not a good fit for a foster youth organization event, but a "County fair" or "Lego" themed party might be.

Those that host annual galas routinely rotate themes to provide a new experience for their guests each year. Masquerade balls, Havana Nights, James Bond, and Roaring 20's themes are all common in the gala world because attendees can dress up and have a fun-filled evening. I've often witnessed that guests who dress according to the theme donate more because they are in "character." Of course, you don't have to have a dress-up themed party to raise a lot of money. If done right, you can raise over a million dollars with a great poolside beach bash theme, as well.

THE GUEST LIST

The guest list is a vital component to a financially successful event. In the retail world, when our guests have a wonderful experience, they will return. We all have a favorite restaurant, what makes it your favorite? Is it because the owner greets you and your husband as you walk in? Is it because someone makes you feel special? Chances are it is because there is a personal connection, and you can feel it. In making guest lists for events, nonprofits think bigger is better. After all, the more people who attend, the more money raised, correct? But what if this isn't the case? Consider this scenario.

The night of your big event is only a week away, but there are still 22 tickets available. Nervous there will be empty seats, the team decides to give the tickets away to friends and family members, hoping that they will buy a silent auction item or a centerpiece at least. Hope is NOT a plan! When the data is compiled after the event, the team discovers that of the 22 people who were given tickets, only one spent money at all.

Clearly, hosting the correct people at the event is more important than having full tables or long guest lists. Seat-fillers might be good for a concert or seminar, but they don't work in fundraising. If your attendees do not have the desire to support your cause and/or the financial means to do so, their attendance may be counterproductive to your purpose. After all, you don't want anyone at a table who will talk the others out of donating. This can be done inadvertently through a comment or disinterest. A guest who comments on their inability to donate can infect those sitting at their table. With a week left before the event, there is still time for a few last minute ticket sales to take place, which will help to recoup some of the total cost of putting on the event in the first place.

DETERMINE YOUR EVENT'S PURPOSE TO DETERMINE THE GUEST LIST

As discussed earlier, some events are designed to primarily educate people about the cause, while others are to give people a fun night out with no real fundraising goals in mind. Most events put on by nonprofit organizations, however, are designed to raise funds to carry out the organization's mission. If your purpose is to educate potential donors, then the guest list should primarily be populated with folks new to the cause. If your purpose is to have a "fun night out" (perhaps to get your name out there or to say thank you to your sponsors and donors), your guest list will consist primarily of past sponsors and donors, as well as a few prospective new sponsors and donors. If, however, the purpose of your event is to raise funds, then careful attention should be made to cultivate individuals with the *will* and *means* to donate to the organization.

CULTIVATING THE GUEST LIST

This is arguably the single most important detail of your event. Taking the time to develop and cultivate a guest list can translate into huge financial benefits the night of your event and beyond. Therefore, board members, staff, key volunteers and perennial donors can all get in on the action.

Start by gathering names from the last three years' events. If you use donor software or event software, you can run reports by specific donation levels. By categorizing them, you can target how to approach them. For example, if someone attended and donated at your event three years ago, but has not since then, the conversation might begin with a "Thank you for supporting *Save the Dogs Today* in the past. Our event is coming up soon and we'd love to have you join us." On the other hand, if someone has attended your event every year for the past three years, you might start by saying something like "It's that time of year again, *Save the Dogs Today* is throwing our annual benefit and we'd love to see you again". It's also important to recognize this donor's previous help, so you might also want to consider adding additional text into the invitation such as: "Your donation of XX last year helped us to provide shelter and vet bills for three amazing dogs, all of which have recently found forever homes. This would not have happened without your help, so again thank you (insert donor's name)".

Next, organize a brainstorming session. Ask key stakeholders to create a list of ten to fifteen of their associates who have never been to the event. Then, ask them to call their list of people and invite them to attend the event as a paying guest or perhaps at a board member's sponsored table. Possible places to find potential guests and donors include:

- Company vendor lists: Either from your organization's contacts or board and sponsor contacts.

- Personal vendor lists: Your realtor, your loan officer, the owner of your hair salon, or owner of your lawn service. The key here is the "owner" of the company, or the stakeholders.

- Service club members: Fellow members of service organizations like Rotary, Civitan, Kiwanis, Knights of Columbus and other similar organizations are good candidates as they are already community minded.

- Professional Organizations: Networking groups, roundtables, associations and other groups where professionals gather.

SAVE THE DATE

Once you have your guest list completed, send out the teams to share the news and begin asking donors to attend.

The two critical aspects of the save the date are the design and the method of launch. If used properly the save the date can really make an impact on your event and streamline your registration/invitation process.

If you've been on an event planning committee then you know ticket sales are a critical piece. The dream of having a sellout event makes for a smoother prep for silent auction, table placement, and creates a realistic opportunity to hit your fundraising goals.

With that in mind the way to use a save the date can be something as simple as a well-designed postcard that then becomes an image that you send through your email marketing and social media to an invitation to the kick-off party where the theme is revealed.

The design of the save the date is critical to accomplish four things:

1. Excite the recipient about your event.

2. Reveal the theme in order to create a buzz.

3. Gently remind sponsors and underwriters that you have reached out to that it's getting close and you want their logos on the upcoming marketing.

In fact, if you have a few sponsors who have already stepped up, be sure to include their logos and a little note that says sponsorship available.

4. Share the WHY. Let people know what funds raised from this event will impact.

THE BEST SAVE THE DATES HAVE:

- Images and bold font/typeface
- Large print (remember donors are average age 62)
- Highlights of the "fun stuff" that will be happening at your event. Music, food and silent auction are expected. Instead, mention the magician, dunk tank or axe throwing to get people excited!

- A website where they can learn more

- The date tickets will be available for sale

- A pre-sale price for tickets and an early bird ticket cut off date

- Be bold, colorful, and stick to the theme (make it quick and easy to read)

- The event title and tagline in parentheses

INVITATIONS

Most people are uncomfortable talking about money, so the most effective way to get a new person to attend an event for a cause is by having someone they know and trust share a personal story about why they love this organization and why it means so much to them, followed by an invitation to attend. Additionally, phone calls and personal invitations from board members can be a great way to get people to attend your event; these calls should be made approximately four weeks out from the event—after initial invitations have been sent out. While calling can be an effective method for inviting people to your event, please note, however, that cold calling is not an effective way to cultivate long term supporters.

Each board member might consider offering to host coffee or happy hour with invitees where they share the mission. Another option is to host a pre-event gathering or kick-off party, where you invite each member on the list for appetizers and beverages. While there, they hear from board members and beneficiaries of the organization, discussing why this mission is so vital to the community. Thus, you have created the perfect opportunity to invite them to attend the main event and to have the opportunity to support this vital cause for themselves.

THE KICK-OFF PARTY

When you are negotiating the contract with the venue for your event, ask them to include a kick off party on a Tuesday or Thursday evening with hosted hors d'oeuvres and cocktails. Most hotels will consider underwriting this event if they are working with nonprofits, particularly if it's a slow time/day. They can use one of their less popular spaces for the venue, and if you think about it from the hotel's perspective it's a low-cost event which would be worth hosting to land a $25,000 - $75,000 contract.

This is a particularly effective strategy for large, gala-type events. If your event venue won't agree to include a kick off party, host a cocktail party at a board member or donor's home, at your facility if you have one, or other location fitting to your cause. Invite known and potential donors to enjoy some appetizers and drinks while mingling with other like-minded individuals. This is your opportunity to educate these important supporters about the mission, direction, and progress of the organization. You can show a video or have a client or board member speak. Just remember to keep it brief, classy and professional. Inviting people to an advance event lets them know how valuable they are to you and the organization. They feel like they are part of a special group. You might even consider offering to have them pick their VIP table or auction off a special item that guests will only have access to at this kick-off event. This reinforces the idea of exclusivity, gets them excited for the main event, and prepares them to donate. Consider inviting your auctioneer, they can really impact the event, meet some donors and build relationships early. Go BIG on this VIP shindig!

COMMUNICATING EXPECTATIONS

It is not uncommon for table sponsors to fill their tables with friends, family members, and employees. For example, a car dealership sponsors your event each year and in return, they receive a table with all of the corresponding tickets to your event to give away at their leisure. They then give their tickets out to employees so they can enjoy a night out on the town as a perk. Although everyone has a great time, the people they invited are not there to donate funds.

Therefore, it is important you take the time to respectfully communicate expectations upfront about the event to your sponsors, and if you do, you may just find you see the difference in the sums collected for your organization that evening.

REAL LIFE EXAMPLE

Make it fun; make it a competition:

A youth-oriented nonprofit organization we work with takes their fundraising very seriously, raising over one million dollars in a single evening every year. What's more, their approach to achieving this goal is actually pretty simple. Each year the board decides collectively that they each will be a Table Captain and take responsibility for inviting people to their tables who have the means to generate a certain amount per table by the end of the evening. This originally started at $2,000 per table, but over the years has grown to $10,000 per table. In fact, it has even become a contest between the board members to see who can bring in the most money each year via the most successful table.

THE TICKET TRAP

All of this having been said, there are some situations that arise which will still make you consider giving some tickets away for free. Should you decide to give tickets away, however, we urge you to do so thoughtfully. Consider choosing individuals who may become donors in the future or associates of people already involved. Appropriate uses of free tickets might be to repair a damaged donor or sponsor relationship, to have civic leaders in attendance to build credibility, or to provide exposure to members of the press. When tickets are given away to friends and family members, use the data after the event to determine the effectiveness of those decisions for planning next year.

Remember, the time invested in creating a list of potential guests, in cultivating those guests, and in tracking the data afterward will help your organization improve the fiscal outcomes for your next event, and develop long-term donor relationships that are key to the success of the organization's mission.

THE VENUE

Choosing the correct venue is vital when creating an experience because it sets the scene for the entire event by evoking different feelings and moods for a total experience. Venues vary widely which can inspire creativity to enhance your event's message, theme, and audience. A unique site can be a draw of its own for guests. Some ideas include wineries, airport hangars, private estates, unusual parks, ranches, museums, universities, sports parks, cargo planes or on the beach.

The size and shape of the venue will often affect the event outcome. Think about the flow of the room, visibility of the stage, and the ability of the emcee and auctioneer to interact with your guests. Take, for example, an event I attended recently at a golf course with a room shaped like a football field. There was a great flow in terms of movement. The shape, however, presented significant challenges for the auctioneer to connect with all of the guests visually and emotionally. Anytime the auctioneer faced one group of people, his back was turned to another. While this is not an insurmountable issue, the layout required additional staff as spotters, (or professional floor auctioneers) in order for the auctioneer to truly engage and interact with the guests.

A critical concern for a successful auction and gala is whether it is an indoor or outdoor facility, and the seasonal weather issues of that location. What time does the sun go down? Is there a wind that blows through at a particular time? Does the temperature drop significantly after dark? Are there sprinklers set to go off at any specific time? For an evening event, walk the property after dark to ensure you've taken all the factors into consideration. Furthermore, if you are going to hire a professional benefit auctioneer, we recommend consulting with him or her before signing the contract to ensure it is the right venue for your specific goals.

After you've chosen your venue, you then need to negotiate your venue contract. This will probably be the most complicated contract you will negotiate throughout planning your entire event, but it is also vitally important to the event's overall success. Event planners can save you big money here, as they often have existing relationships and know what to ask for in the negotiations. It's definitely a skillset. Some points to consider when negotiating your venue contract:

- Do they have in-house catering or can you bring in your own caterer?

- What options are provided for meals? Buffet, table service, accommodations for special diets? Do they offer reduced or alternate meals for children, if applicable?

- What is the minimum order? What is the cut-off date/deadline for changing meal counts?

- What is included in the per-person price? Is that only the meal or does it include linens and cutlery/plates/glasses as well?

- Are servers included in the price? How many are provided?

- Do they have in-house audio visual (AV) or should you contract with an outside agency? Are you allowed to contract outside of the venue for AV?

- What is the sound system set-up for your space? Can it be upgraded? What is the cost? Again, are you allowed to bring in a sound/AV company if the venue's system is not adequate for your event needs?

- Is there an extra charge for Wifi, additional electrical outlets, etc.? Wi-Fi needs – if you are using software to run check-in, check-out, and sales, can you be hardwired or on Wi-Fi – is it included or extra? This can be a HUGE expense if not negotiated early on. Are you conducting a mobile bidding event? You may need guest access to the system if you are in the basement. You will need to work with your mobile bidding provider and a tech at the venue on bandwidth requirements and test the system before the event. Do they provide an area for check-in/check-out? If not, is there an additional cost for setting this up?

- Do they have a green room area for volunteers? What is the cost to feed your volunteers?

- Will an event coordinator be on site the day or evening of the event to assist with last-minute issues? Can you set up days in advance?

- If you are bringing in your own wine, is there a corkage fee?

- What is the cost for open bar versus cash bar? What is the cost per bartender?

- Is there valet parking? If parking is a distance away, is there a shuttle available for those with mobility issues? Are there other events at the venue that day like a wedding that will put strain on the valet staff?

- What signage will the venue provide?

- Do they provide any marketing or advertising on your behalf?

- Are there discounts for holding it earlier or on an alternate day like a Tuesday or Thursday?

- Are there any sponsorship opportunities through the venue itself?

- What is the ease of loading in and loading out?

- Are there time restraints for setup and teardown? Can you get in the room the day prior?

- What is the venue insurance requirements—amounts, liability, aggregate?

Note, too, that developing a relationship with the venue's Events Manager beyond your contract can be quite beneficial. As they get to know you and your cause, they will be able to make suggestions that enhance your next event based on past experience. In addition, they may be able to help guide potential donors or sponsors your way when they see a natural fit.

Booking the date for the venue a year in advance is the industry standard. This should also kick off the timeline in terms of the amount of time it takes to plan an event. If Darren could have it his way, we would start planning 18 months prior to the event, with a stewardship piece that thanks the donors for coming to the gala six months before with a photo and a feel good note about the impact. For Michelle, this belongs on the year prior's event timeline in the post-event section. Either way—potato potato, tomato, tomato—it's an absolute best practice we'd highly recommend. And booking the auctioneer and non-theme dependent entertainment well in advance is another must-do.

THE PROFESSIONAL "ASK-ER"

One of the most important decisions you make about your charity event is whether or not you hire a Benefit Auctioneer Specialist (BAS). Just like event planners, there are auctioneers that specialize in many different types of auctions, including autos, antiques, estates, and art. Benefit auctions are a unique type of auction, however. Rather than people bidding higher because of the material benefit, at a benefit auction, you are inspiring people to bid higher because they are giving, not just getting. It is the act of generosity that drives a benefit auction. Therefore, it takes a different mentality and skill set to successfully facilitate a benefit auction.

Benefit Auctioneer Specialists (BAS) do not just sell auction items. They act as an ambassador for your cause. They are the spokesperson for your mission the day of your event and have the ability to put your mission in the spotlight. A Fundraising Auctioneer helps build awareness of your cause by interacting with your guests and learning why they are attending. The guests need to know your auctioneer is a part of your actual team—and not just a vendor who is asking for money and selling trips. If you can do this, it will have a large pay off every time. Throughout the cocktail hour and/or silent auction, the Benefit Auctioneer is mingling with guests, developing relationships, and finding out what makes their hearts swoon. A qualified and experienced Fundraising Auctioneer also entertains the crowd and keeps them excited about bidding and being generous to your cause. Additionally, a BAS doesn't just show up on the night of the event: he or she is with you and your team every step of the way.-

Because of all this, it is important to take the decision whether or not to hire a BAS seriously. It is also important to note it can actually end up costing your organization a lot of money if you choose not to get a BAS. A free and/or inexperienced auctioneer isn't going to know how to work the crowd and excite them and raise bids. They aren't going to be able to keep track of bids the way a professional auctioneer would be able to, and they will likely end up missing bids all together. Plus, if the auctioneer decides to drink at your event, they could end up damaging your brand and decreasing donation dollars by telling a distasteful joke or by talking politics for example. A certified BAS is an investment, often easily measurable with "ROA" (or "Return on Auctioneer") as a colleague once said. Your auctioneer can often pay for themselves time and time again, and it pays for you to make sure you're hiring a professional.

CHAPTER 9
FUNDRAISING MATH

Many organizations we speak to decide to host an event and put it on the calendar. They start gathering committee members and volunteers, but they often forget the most important step: goals and budgets are the lifeline of a nonprofit organization. They create the benchmark for your organization to measure success, and they set the stage for future fundraising efforts. Whether this is your first fundraiser or your nonprofit's 30th annual gala, there is no substitute for having a detailed, well-thought-out and board-approved budget. Each special event you host should be part of a larger comprehensive development plan. Each event must have its own specific fundraising goal.

For example, with an annual budget of $500,000, nonprofit XYZ hosts three events each year and an annual giving campaign that includes an end of year "ask" with a late winter mailing. Each one of these is part of a larger development calendar and therefore has its own individual budget. The budget for each will include revenue (projected sponsorship and straight donations) and expenses—including the cost of mailing, printing, postage, event fees, acknowledgment, and staff time.

When setting your goals, answer the following three simple questions:

1. Does your overall fundraising goal cover the program expenses as well as any administration and staff fees?

2. Do you have projected revenues and expenses for *each* profit source at your event?

3. Are the goals you're setting for each revenue source based on last year's performance, with a 10 to 15% increase?

OVERHEAD EXPENSES VS. PROGRAM COSTS

Knowing that the "gold standard" is to have 25% or less of your funds raised cover the expenses of your organization, it is imperative to consider your annual budget as a first step. What does it cost to run the ship? Rent, staff, office supplies, marketing expenses, technology and phones are all basic overhead expenses. These are merely the foundation costs required to keep the organization operating and functioning, regardless of what programs are being run. Then there are expenses around the services you provide, which are your program costs. For example, if your nonprofit offers job training opportunities for the homeless population, what are the costs of that individual program on its own? This is *not* part of the 25% overhead in terms of budget.

SETTING AN EVENT FUNDRAISING GOAL

Each special event you host should be part of a larger, comprehensive fundraising development plan. Your event must have a specific fundraising goal which should be measurable, attainable, and time-based.

- What are the specific needs? (i.e. like a new gym, parking lot, expand outreach)? How much will it cost?

- How many people will be attending?

- How much does each attendee need to spend to reach our goal?

- What donation opportunities will your event provide? What is the specific goal of each one?

- What sort of incentives will you provide to entice giving at the event?

Your initial investment, overhead, and operational costs will vary according to the size and type of an event, and often is in direct relation to the amount of money per person you have set for your goal.

Let's imagine you want to net $100,000 from an event and plan on having 400 people in attendance. Many organizations make the critical mistake of dividing the amount they want to raise by the number of *attendees*, which seems logical enough. But in reality, most of those 400 people in traditional gala event settings are there as part of a *couple*. And when you look at human behavior and the data, you'll see that couples don't typically donate as individuals— they donate together as one unit (or as a household if this were a family event). That makes a HUGE difference in terms of the budget implications. If you based your event on the assumption that there are 400 people who would be donating, you'd be budgeting that each person would need to donate $250 to hit the $100,000 goal. You'd set your sights on making sure the auction and other revenue streams within the event catered to having people spend at least $250; all night long you'd be feeling good as you watched people hitting that mark, thinking you're on track—*until* you sit down and count the money the next day. And then you'd be sitting there, scratching your head in confusion and wondering what the heck happened. You were watching people with your own two eyes, donating right on target, yet how could you have been so far off the goal? In reality, you'd need to be asking people to donate $500 to hit the goal, since you'd really only be pulling from a donor pool of 200 couples, NOT 400 individuals.

REVENUE STREAMS

Choosing the revenue streams for your event is an important part of the planning process and can really affect the success of your fundraiser. While the classics like live auctions and silent auctions are always at the top of the list, we encourage you to think differently and look for ways to shake things up while streamlining the amount of resources required to run the event. For example, there is plenty of data that shows that online auctions can bring in 30% more revenue than a silent auction and best of all they require almost half the number of hours to plan and execute. A silent auction does work better for some markets than others, and when you look at the math it's easy to make a decision to possibly move it online or eliminate it and focus on the other fundraising activities during the reception hours.

There are so many creative revenue streams available, with new ones being added to the list all the time. To ensure we continue to give you the most relevant and up to date information even well into the future, we've opted to put the list of what's new, hot and current in terms of creative event revenue streams on our website at fundraisingadvisors.org.

THE TRUE COST OF FUNDRAISING

Now that we have a general sense of the "per wallet" formula versus the "per person" one, let's take a look at the specifics of fundraising math.

Let's imagine that an organization has a fundraising goal of $250,000 for the year.

Their annual Gala net revenue averages about $150,000. They also host two small cocktail party fundraising events each year with a collective goal of $75,000 and a few smaller third party events that bring in around $25,000 total.

Let's take a deep dive into the Gala math to see what it will take to reach that $150,000 goal.

First up, the basics.

$150,000 plus 30% for overhead = $195,000 (the national average is 50% for overhead but Eventology says that is crazy high!)

Add another $5,000 to be safe because your best friend's buddy's wife just may not come through on the "free" DJ or event planner. And as we've said, there's always a fee for free.

So now we need to raise $200,000. Divide that by 250 guests and we need each donor/guest to bring $800. Realistically, however it's not

250 guests—we need to count the wallets/purses in the room. It's a safe assumption that most guests will bring their partners or spouses, which means that we are now needing to actually count on $1,600 per couple/household as the right figure.

First question: Do we really have 250 donors in our database that will invest $800 each or $1,600 per couple? If yes, please call us, we want to meet your donors!

Back to reality (for most of us). $45,000 is the budget to spend. That's it! No more, no less. Knowing that the expense should be 30% overall, here is how expenses might look for this organization:

$50 to $90 per person for food and the venue - $22,500

Hosted bar - $5,000 (that's assuming two drinks per guest at $10/drink)

Entertainment and décor - $10,000

Audio/Video - $5,000

Event planner - $5,000

Auctioneer - $3,500 - $7,500 (You can definitely find one who works for food and drinks, but do you really want them to be them to be your fundraiser? How invested will they be with your organization? This should be more than a two hour job. It takes months to plan.)

Marketing - $5,000 (Yep! You need to get the word out and print all kinds of stuff. That fancy color printer in the office probably just isn't going to cut it.)

Staff time - $20,000 (This is based on a percentage of salaries during gala prep)

Grand total for expenses? $76,000! Busted already, and we haven't even bought dessert!

Don't panic. Just change the math—*and* get some sponsors. You've GOT THIS!

All right, back at it. Let's add that additional $31,000 to our original $45,000 budget for a new goal of $231,000 or $930 per guest.

So how do we get there?

Sponsorships need to equal $100,000:

$35k - Title sponsor

$20k - VIP reception sponsor

$10k - Entertainment sponsor

$10k - Champagne and Wine sponsor

$10k - Silent/online auction sponsor

$6k - Live auction sponsor

$5k - Paddle raise sponsor

$5k - Valet sponsor

$2,500 - Non-alcoholic beverage sponsor

$2,500 - Centerpiece sponsor

If you can get one of each of these, you're at $106,000! Only $125,000 to go ($500 per guest).

You will need eight to ten Live Auction items that average $2,500 each. You want some for $1,000 and one or two that can bring in $5,000 for a live auction goal of $25,000.

When determining the number of Silent Auction items you need, the following formula should be applied:

250 guests divided by two = 125 couples/"wallets"

125 wallets divided by 1/4 = you'll want approximately 30 items in the silent auction

Remember that silent auction items will yield about 50% of their value, so—in order to reach $25,000 in profit, you're going to need around $50,000 in auction items.

If you're keeping up with the math, we are still just a bit short on the goal. $75,000 short to be exact.

Now—let's move onto the largest impact portion of your event: The ASK! We need just $300 per guest, and most events can achieve this with solid pre-planning, the right people in the room, and a great team on board. You'll need and want to craft an amazing impact message to get into the hearts and minds of your donors, guests and volunteers. With a well thought out event timeline, we can raise the additional funds AND leave the guests inspired and motivated to support your organization at the event and into the future.

We are SO close. With the support of key donors, one pre-planned gift of $10,000 to kick off the ASK and 3 to 5 pledges of $5,000, we are nearing the goal and the majority of the guests have not yet participated. It's time to ask them *all* to raise their hands to fund the dreams and future of your organization. With a few gifts at each ask—$2,500, $1,000, $500, $250 and down to the last ask at $100—BAM!!

Goal hit! Congratulations!

Hang on. We mentioned ticket sales earlier: the event was $100 to attend, and you sold 250 tickets. Let's add $25,000 to the total. $255,000 for the win!

Regardless of your organization's budget and goal, the process needs to be as thorough and well thought out as possible. Do the math, run the numbers, and know well ahead of time what your plan of action will be to make that a reality.

CHAPTER 10
BEFORE THE EVENT

SETTING THE TIMELINE

The timeline for your event is a critical component of your success, and could be the element that makes or breaks the day. The timeline we present here is a sound order of events based on over 20 years of research and data collection, in chronological order. Three great uses of the timeline include:

1. The event timeline can be a shared tool for volunteer committee members, the Executive Director, and development staff. If used in a shared technology, for instance, members of the committee can track their duties and update tasks as completed.

2. A timeline can act as a roadmap for brand new staff members, event coordinators, and co-chairs—in addition to providing continuity and a documented history from year to year. Someone who may have stepped into the event for the first time can rely on the timeline from the last year in order to create the timeline for this year's gala.

3. The timeline helps track the amount of hours and time spent in active fundraising. This is important because many nonprofits fail to evaluate the true cost of fundraising—particularly around events—which should include volunteer and staff time. So even though the hard cost of a gala may be $113 per person in expenses, a nonprofit should also take into consideration the hourly time (both paid and volunteer) when calculating the total cost of an event. The timeline is an essential resource in tracking tasks and the amount of time associated with each.

In this sample timeline it's important to point out some key, time-sensitive pieces that can lead to a home run event, whether you're planning a 5K fun run, a chili-cookoff or a golf tournament.

Preparation for your fundraising event should begin twelve months in advance and incorporate all facets: setting goals, selecting committees, creating and sending invitations, ticket sales, marketing, securing auction items, sponsors and underwriters, event timeline, run of show, scripts, and more.

Sponsorship opportunities, brochures, and communications should be sent out eight to nine months prior to your event. This will allow proper time for individual follow up, sponsorship benefits to be established, and marketing pieces like the logo and website updates to be added to the marketing timeline. Even though this makes sense practically, many nonprofits fail to do this early enough. Take budgets into consideration and realize that businesses plan this year for next year's budget, including marketing and charitable giving. Make the invitation to participate intriguing and unique. The sponsorship ask is an opportunity to be part of something fun, exciting, and something the business and attendees will benefit from. Do your research. Find charitable businesses and foundations that support like-events or organizations and find the decision maker's name (and favorite coffee/drink if possible).

"We would like to offer you a premier opportunity to participate in our Annual Benefit Golf Tournament With 288 guests and a reach of over 4500—in terms of marketing, social media, and PR. We are certain your sponsorship dollars will be an excellent investment and carry the benefit of the tax deduction right along with it."

Which brings me to my favorite quote: "Lack of 'no' means maybe."

Unfortunately, this has backfired on me with my own children, but that's for a different story. Many nonprofits we work with are frustrated because they send one, two, three or even five follow-up emails to sponsorship request letters, plus a phone call, and don't even get a return phone call. Much like the typical sales funnel, it's a seven point touch matrix for a sponsorship ask.

1 — Send Sponsor Packet

2 — Follow-up phone call

3 — Follow-up email

4 — Office visit/fly by

5 — Send save the date with a personal note

6 — Follow-up email with a deadline

7 — No reply = break-up email

In fact, if you hit the sixth and have not received a reply of "no" then it's time for the famous "break up email". This is honestly one of my favorite tools and has been extremely effective in securing donors and sponsorship for my events:

"Dear Henry,

Since I have not heard from you, I will assume you are not interested in our Annual Benefit Golf Tournament sponsor opportunities as we had hoped. I am sure you have been busy and I want to be respectful of your time.

I will not bother you further.

Thank you,

Michelle Gilmore

This email is magic and will get a response. It may be a "no," but at least then you will have your answer.

THE 12 MONTH TIMELINE

Let's start by charting out a year-long production timeline. Even if your team is a team of one initially, taking the time to look ahead and see all the steps involved in bringing a successful charity event to fruition can save you tremendous stress later and make for a far more successful event. It will also define areas where you need to recruit volunteers and other support help. Sharing this timeline with your Board of Directors and staff/volunteers can also help rally the troops and raise the sense of urgency. It is easy to be lulled into a daze by the idea that the fundraiser is a year away and you have plenty of time!

10-12 Months in advance

☐ Define the purpose for your event

☐ Select a date and venue. Consider space needs, parking, WiFi, community calendars, popular dates, holidays and major sporting events.

☐ Establish a budget including fundraising goals and revenue streams

☐ Hire a professional benefit auctioneer specialist

☐ Select an event chairperson who is well connected and has strong leadership skills

☐ Establish overall committee names and responsibilities

☐ Research auction software: Which solutions can help streamline your event?

☐ Develop a general marketing plan

☐ Explore the organization's donor database to develop the invitation list

☐ Develop underwriting and sponsorship levels and benefits

☐ Research and identify past and potential sponsors and underwriters

☐ Identify a Volunteer Coordinator

7-10 Months in advance

- [ ] Choose an event theme (the volunteer co-chairs of your event should have a say in all of the details that many deem to be the "fun stuff," like choosing the theme)

- [ ] Recruit and establish committees

- [ ] Develop the team captain and team member contact lists

- [ ] Begin acquiring underwriters and sponsors

- [ ] Develop donation forms

- [ ] Create a volunteer waiver form to legally protect liability of the organization from accidents and other incidents

- [ ] Detail the marketing plan and calendar

    - [ ] Create graphics for theme

    - [ ] Hire a graphic designer, if needed

    - [ ] Develop save-the-date announcements

    - [ ] Develop promotional emails

    - [ ] Develop and send solicitation letters and in-kind donation forms

- [ ] Continue refining and adding to invitation list

- [ ] Conduct a procurement team meeting

- [ ] Hire a professional audio-visual company

- [ ] Secure benefit auction software if appropriate

5-7 Months in advance

- ☐ Meet with Committee Team Captains to develop committee plans

- ☐ Interview caterers and entertainment if necessary*

- ☐ Select a Master of Ceremonies and/or announcer

- ☐ Begin auction and event promotion

  - ☐ Begin the invitation design

  - ☐ Mail the Save-the-Date announcements

  - ☐ Develop event specific website, domain and hashtags

  - ☐ Create signature tag for staff and volunteers to use in email

  - ☐ Ensure event is posted on your organization's website

  - ☐ Create evite and Facebook event

  - ☐ Write, distribute press release about the event with pictures & PSA

- ☐ Continue acquisition of underwriters and sponsors

- ☐ Begin to brainstorm the story for the Special Appeal

- ☐ Establish a firm deadline for acquisition of auction items

- ☐ Track acquisition of auction items and start collecting images

3 -5 Months in advance

☐ Post updates with hashtags on social media and websites

☐ Create the ability to sell tickets and sponsorships online

☐ Continue to solicit auction items; check with the State Attorney General's office regarding your specific state laws and whether you need to notify your guests about consignment items or not

☐ Consult with auctioneer on floor plan and event layout

☐ Consult with auctioneer on registration, cashiering, and auction claim & removal process

☐ Consult with audio-visual company about needs for the event

☐ Continue procuring underwriters and sponsors

☐ Solidify story and identify donation levels for Special Appeal

☐ Film video for Special Appeal

☐ Begin securing preplanned major gift for Special Appeal

☐ Secure date for volunteer thank you party

1-3 Months in advance

- ☐ Mail the invitations

- ☐ Distribute press release that highlights charity and its success

- ☐ Arrange local radio interviews of founders or beneficiaries

- ☐ Distribute promotional emails and newsletters

- ☐ Promote event on social media once a week

- ☐ Invite friends through Facebook event page, encourage committee to do same

- ☐ If budget allows – boost post through Facebook

- ☐ Review "likes" on boost post and invite those who have not liked, friended or followed organizational FB page to like – build your audience

- ☐ Promote event on website home page and event websites

- ☐ Finalize sponsorships

- ☐ Prepare or order bid paddles or cards and bid sheets

- ☐ Create a phone bank team of volunteers to call or email invitees

- ☐ Secure and train Table Captains

- ☐ Develop layout of the seating and auction displays

- ☐ Begin to develop auction catalog

- ☐ Create Live Auction slideshow

- [ ] Design sponsor recognitions

- [ ] Confirm with entertainment, Master of Ceremonies, sound company, and caterer

- [ ] Create live and silent auction display boards

- [ ] Finalize checkin and checkout procedures

- [ ] Finalize auction item pickup procedures

- [ ] Begin to create guest list and seating charts

- [ ] Begin to write the Run of Show script for the event

2 Weeks in advance

- [ ] Schedule a phone conference with your auctioneer to review the catalog and sequence of live auction items

- [ ] Create needed certificates for auction items; verify expiration dates and fine print on all procured certificates

- [ ] Create list of volunteer assignments and schedule

- [ ] Create needed signage

- [ ] If using auction software, assign items to packages and sections

- [ ] Finalize Run of Show script and schedule a dress rehearsal

- [ ] Create floor plan for silent auction

- [ ] Communicate with speakers; ensure they are comfortable with their part

- ☐ Confirm key volunteers for the day after the event (answering phones, processing donations, etc.)

- ☐ Continue to encourage attendance

- ☐ Enter last minute guests

1 Week before

- ☐ Review final catalog and script with your auctioneer

- ☐ Ensure all silent auction items have package numbers attached

- ☐ Assign guests to tables; provide for unexpected guests in table assignments

- ☐ Provide final guest count to venue and caterer

- ☐ Finalize number of volunteer spotters/ringmen for the live auction (one for every 125 people in the crowd)

- ☐ Confirm setup for computers and printers at venue; test Wi-Fi capabilities

- ☐ Hold volunteer training

- ☐ Print bid sheets if using auction software

- ☐ Organize all auction certificates in numerical order by bid number

1 Day before

- ☐ Print catalog addendum if needed

- ☐ Print final schedule and script; distribute as needed

- ☐ Deliver all items to venue if possible

- ☐ Ensure all live and silent auction items are entered into auction software

- ☐ Review guest list and ensure all guests are entered into event software

- ☐ Hold dress rehearsal, if possible

Day of Event

- ☐ Sound and lighting check

    - ☐ Make sure video presentations work with equipment provided

    - ☐ Make sure cordless microphones all have new, fresh batteries

- ☐ Match up bid sheets to auction items

- ☐ Set-up auction

- ☐ Hold dress rehearsal (unless it is an early event, in which case do one day before event)

- ☐ Hold a staff and volunteer meeting several hours before the event to ensure all roles and responsibilities are clear and to answer any questions

☐ During the event, be as relaxed, calm and joyful as you can be, and accept that with any large event there is likely something that will go wrong. You've done your absolute best to plan out every detail, and now it's time to empower your team to do their best when executing, and let go of the rest. The single most important thing to remember is just to focus on creating a wonderful experience for your donors and guests!

RUN OF SHOW SCRIPT

Just as a twelve month timeline is crucial to success, so is your Run of Show script.

From event setup through the tear-down, the Run of Show is the written document that explains to the 'behind-the-scenes' organizers the detailed sequence of events planned. It is the master document that contains all of the critical components of the event.

When preparing your Run of Show script, be sure to detail the exact timing for each part of the event, right down to when plates should be cleared between courses. What time will your first volunteer arrive? When does the bartender set up? What time is the sound and lighting check? The more you can plan for ahead of time, the smoother the event will run for everyone.

While every event will be different, visit fundraisingadvisors.org for a downloadable version of a sample Run of Show script we created for a client to give you some idea of the level of detail that should be included when preparing yours.

THIRD-PARTY VENDORS

Finding Your Backstage Crew

There are many avenues to find qualified and insured/bonded vendors for your event. The local Chamber of Commerce will have a list of local, civic-minded businesses from which to choose. You can also ask the venue coordinator for suggestions, as they often have relationships with vendors who have demonstrated professionalism over time. Some venues may require you to choose only from their list of preferred vendors. If not, online review sites can also be used to gather ideas and input for where to find potential new members. Websites of recommended vendors can offer references and vendors who sponsor or donate their services to other groups; this can provide a profile of the competitive landscape within a pool of potential vendors. Always perform your due diligence on any vendor by calling their references.

Setting Expectations

Take the time to outline your expectations for your crew in writing. We strongly suggest you include a "no drinking" policy in your contracts as well as in your volunteer agreements and waivers. Under no circumstances should a vendor or volunteer be drinking alcoholic beverages while on the job. This can spell disaster for an event. Be sure to outline other expectations, as well—such as time of arrival and departure, manner of dress for the evening, and ensure your people sign off on the document, in addition to signing a volunteer waiver form. That way, everyone is on the same page from the beginning.

Caterers

If your event is being held in a location where you will need to hire an outside caterer, there are many factors to consider in choosing the right one. First, before taking the plunge and actually hiring a caterer, take the time to check their references, online reviews, and venue recommendations; many events have been sidelined when the food showed up late or cold. Other important questions to ask include:

- What is your refund and cancellation policy?
- What is included in the per-person cost?
- Is setup, teardown, gratuity, and labor included in the per--person cost?
- What is the policy for leftovers?
- Do you provide bartenders and/or serve alcohol?
- Who carries the ABC (Alcoholic Beverage Control) license—your organization or the caterer?
- If permits are needed, do you provide those?
- Are you licensed and insured?
- Can you accommodate dietary restrictions even if last minute on the day of the event?
- Where do you source your food?
- How many servers will there be? How will they be dressed?
- Who is the point person for the evening?
- Do you provide food tastings?
- Do you provide all of the plates/glasses/cutlery/linens?
- Do you handle cleanup? What is included in the cleanup?

- Do you charge for including us on your certificate of additional insured for the venue?

Bar Services

If the caterer does not provide their own bartending service and you're planning on serving alcoholic beverages, choose your vendor carefully. Again, do your research before hiring and pay close attention to prices and fees, as there can be many hidden charges. Things to consider when hiring a bar service:

- What is the bartender to guest ratio?
- Do they provide portable bars? Do they have custom bar designs for themed events?
- Can you provide the alcohol or do they? Is there a corkage fee if you do?
- Do they provide all of the mixers and garnishes?
- What happens to the leftover alcohol?
- How are you charged for the liquor if they provide it? By drink? By ounce?
- Can they create a specialized drink menu for your event?
- Are their bartenders licensed in the state?
- Are they insured?
- Will there be a tip jar? Who receives the tips at the end of the evening?
- What are the Certificate of additional insured requirements of the venue (amount and liability)?

Audio Visual (AV)

It is important that you work closely with your AV team to determine how they can support what you are doing. Outline expectations and needs clearly to determine if they can meet them. Additionally, identify what equipment (if any) will be provided by the venue and what your Audio Visual team will need to bring themselves. For example, will you be live streaming the event? Will you need an outdoor projector and screen? Will you need microphones, and if so—what type?

Your Audio Visual team will also be responsible for cueing up your music and videos. If you are planning on using video as part of your message, be sure to work with the AV team to ensure it is audible and visible to all guests in the venue. Also confirm with the AV team what format they need to produce the best video results. An experienced AV team can actually help increase revenue at your event.

PRO TIP
Adapting your audio/visual vision to avert disaster

I once worked an event where the chair had a specific vision involving showing a touching video to the guests during the event. The problem was, they were so intent on making this happen and ignored all the reasons it wasn't a great idea. You see, the event was to take place at an outdoor venue on a June evening. This meant issues with sun glare and sound would be no small obstacle to overcome. Fortunately, the event planner was able to do a walkthrough of the venue with the AV vendor prior to any final decisions, and with his input was able to help the chair understand why this specific vision was not logistically or financially feasible. Because of the time of sundown and the shape of the property, they would be unable to use one large outdoor screen. Instead the AV company recommended four large screen televisions costing $3,500. There was simply no room in the budget for the expense. In the end, previewing the area with experts prevented the guests from not being able to see or hear the video, saved money, and helped to avoid a frustrating experience for all concerned.

Points to consider when choosing your AV vendor:

- Have they worked in this venue before? 8 out of 10 times the venue will say the sound and light systems are perfect. They will say there is no need to bring anything. The problem is 8 out of 10 times they are wrong. You should always consult with your AV team to make sure they have everything they need, especially if they have never worked at your particular venue before.

- Can they tour the venue with you ahead of time?

- Have they worked with an auctioneer before?

- Is the sound check included in the contract price?

- Do they provide a DJ? If so, do they have experience working at charity benefits?

- Check references for their capability and professionalism.

When it comes to the event, it is critical that the venue sound system is robust enough so that the entire audience can hear. If they can't hear the story, they can't be moved by the story. If the sound system provided by the venue is not of high quality, it is worth the extra investment to rent (or purchase) a high quality sound system. No matter if your speakers will be appearing live or by video (or both), the sound system is extremely important. Many venues will sell you by saying they've got a sound system. Perhaps it does sound great if you're going to a seminar and nobody's talking except for that one person, but when you're in a fundraising event where guests are having a few drinks and people are catching up with friends, you can be sure that nobody is going to be quiet and listen to every word you're going to say. Your sound system has to be over and above whatever the volume of the room is and you have to have the ability to go higher and higher with a bold, rich sound.

Consider also that often the speakers in the front are so loud, that the people in the front—which are often your biggest donors—have their hands up over their ears because it's too loud and the people in the back can't hear. It is better to have surround-sound speakers on all four corners of the room or eight speakers spaced equally around the room so everybody can hear at the same levels.

Lighting

For a silent auction, mini lamps are a must, especially if you're outside. Even inside, you need to have lighting on the tables for your bid sheets.

Professional lighting will set the tone and create a mood for the evening to match your theme and message. Colors, spotlights, gobos, and lasers enhance the venue and decorations. Be sure to check that your venue has adequate power for all of your lighting needs.

Graphic Design

Investing in professional graphic design for flyers, invitations, programs (if you are printing one or placing online) and even your website, can truly elevate your event and your organization. You want potential donors to view your organization as professional and well-run. Although creating your own printed materials is cheaper, the overall quality and impact is usually not nearly as effective. Professional designers utilize design principles and professional applications to create visuals that evoke the desired emotions and response. Format and sizing for social media, print media, and digital campaigns vary in ways that desktop programs cannot produce without loss of quality. Business people understand there is a cost to doing business, so don't shy away from the investment in good graphic design.

Entertainment

There are many places to find good local inexpensive talent. Although a middle school choir is local and free, it may not be an appropriate match for your event.

Make sure your entertainment matches your theme and message. A veterans-oriented group might feature a patriotic or military group singing; a youth-oriented group might feature young local talent; and a Gatsby-themed night might feature a jazz singer. Additionally, guest speakers are also a form of entertainment. Remember the focus of the event and stay true to that. If the entertainment doesn't add value to the event, or enhance your theme and focus, skip the expense.

One more thing to remember about entertainment: dead air is painful and causes anxiety in people. During the silent auction, consider having someone play instrumental music or have the DJ find themed music to play. During transitions inside the event, provide appropriately themed music to keep the flow going. People are much more likely to stay longer, spend more money, and enjoy themselves more when they are comfortable. Music is an amazing way to make that happen.

Some thoughts to consider when choosing your entertainment and guest speakers:

- How much experience do they have?
- Do they have references they can provide?
- Do they have a website with sample music and/or speeches?
- What is the fee and what does it include?
- How many people are in the set-up crew if any?
- Will they be attending the event and how many seats will they expect?
- What type of sound equipment will they need?
- Will they use any special lighting? Who will provide that?
- Who will do their set up?
- What do they typically wear?

Choosing your entertainment may be far less stressful than determining the other vendors, but make sure the contract clearly outlines compensation and expectations just the same.

Florist/Centerpiece Designer

Flowers are beautiful and timeless, but centerpieces don't always have to be floral arrangements. Centerpieces can be candles, pictures, or a vast array of fun things you can find on Pinterest. Just remember that everything contributes to the theme and message, so staying on point—even with table centerpieces—is important. Centerpieces can also make great additional auction items at the end of the night.

PRO TIP
Too much foliage can lead to less profit

A fundraising "Havana Nights" themed event included all guests dressed in their Cuban and Caribbean attire and having a wonderful time. The centerpieces, however, were a problem. Each table had two large palm fronds placed in a tall vase in the center of the table. While it looked wonderful, with fifty tables in the room, it made it impossible for me as the auctioneer to see the donors and guests; nor could they see the items during the live auction.

If you *are* going to have flowers as your centerpieces, you will most likely be working with a florist. Items to consider when selecting your florist include:

- Can they work within your budget?
- Would they be willing to discount the price for sponsorship benefits?

- Have they worked in this venue before?

- How will the flowers be delivered? Do they pick up?

- Will they provide a sample for you to see before making a final decision?

- Do they charge a delivery fee?

Remember it's not a wedding, it's a fundraiser. Make the centerpieces about the nonprofit. And if you're engaging a benefit auctioneer, remember that he or she will need to be able to make direct eye contact with your guests, so make sure the table decorations do not inhibit this connection.

Consignment Vendors

Using consignment items (items provided to your event by consignment vendors that are considered unique and/or rare and for which a minimum price or reserve must be met) can bring excitement and variety to both your silent and live auctions. From autographed pictures to sports memorabilia to exotic trips, the right consignment items can truly add flair to your event.

While consignment items can be fun, there is a reserve fee (the fee that consignment vendors collect if the item sells), which is an expense. This often "takes money out of the room" that doesn't go to the charity. For example, you may have a guest with a budget to spend up to $10,000 because they love your organization. If they buy an item for $5,000 and it cost the NPO $3,200 to actually buy the trip on consignment, the net proceeds are only $1,800 going to the charity instead of the $5,000 the donor actually donated.

Here are Eventology's pros and cons to using consignment items in your auction, but ultimately it's up to you and your team to decide what's best for your unique event.

Pros:

- Excites the crowd
- Adds something new to your auctions (especially when your typical donations seem to be falling short)
- Increases variety in auction items
- Can be sold multiple times if it is a trip or experience
- You can choose what to sell
- Items can tie in with your theme
- You can select items based on known attendees
- No financial risk; if it doesn't sell, the consignment vendors will simply take it back
- Great for newer organizations which lack widespread support in the community
- Great for people who don't have the time to devote to finding a bunch of auction items
- Can help to identify potential high-end donor candidates
- Is a great way to procure a high-end selection of donor auction items (a feat which is normally really difficult)
- Offers a sponsor the ability to underwrite an item

Cons:

- There is a reserve fee (the fee that consignment vendors collect if the item sells), which is an expense.

- Some states require that you notify your guests if an item is a consignment piece. Be sure to check with the State Attorney General's office regarding your specific state laws on this matter before the auction.

- On occasion, guests are upset when they purchase consignment items because they thought all of the money was going to the cause

- Sometimes trips or experiences sold come with blackout dates

- Can be difficult to clearly communicate what is included in the package being sold

There are some other important points to take under consideration when choosing a consignment vendor as well:

- Is payment due up front?

- Will the items sell and be desirable to your specific audience?

- What is the reputation of the company?

- What is the damage policy?

- What is the return policy?

- Is there a "no sale" fee?

- Do they provide certificates of authenticity?

- Is the item compatible with the event theme and focus?

If after reading all of this and discussing it with your team as well as your auctioneer, you decide to move ahead with using consignment items at your auction, your benefit auctioneer can be a great advisor.

Often he or she will try to limit each event to one or two consignment items to help keep the bottom line protected. Many have a great deal of experience selling consignment items and can guide you through the selection process, so be sure to take advantage of this.

Event Planner

If you are the Executive Director or Development Professional, your life is already filled with 850 details each and every day above and beyond those of your event.

The idea of visualizing something of this magnitude and then being held accountable to the planning of every detail may well make you feel sick to your stomach. This is where a professional event planner can help you. Yes, it is an additional expense, yet you absolutely must consider YOUR time as an expense in the fundraising budget, as well. If your time and mental energy is being taken away from your year-end giving campaign or important donor visits, or if your organization is too small to have a fund development person, then hiring an event planner makes perfect sense. He or she will coordinate with your committees and event chair, take care of all of the details, and communicate with you on a regular basis. Additionally, on the day of the event, the event planner will be the one running around making sure everything is perfect while you arrive looking coiffed and relaxed, ready to interact with donors and enjoy the fruits of your labor. Even if you decide to handle most of the pre-event planning yourself/internally, you may wish to consider bringing on an event planner to manage just the actual event day itself so you can focus fully on maximizing the revenue from the event versus running around dealing with issues that will distract you from the main task at hand.

Regardless of whether long-term or short-term, if you bring on an event planner in any capacity *please* make sure to find one that has specific experience with charity benefits. This is a *much* different event than a wedding or an anniversary party; the goal here is fundraising while showing them a great time—not simply putting on a great time for its own sake.

Event planners often charge their fees in a variety of ways. The two most common are a flat fee up front or a percentage of the total cost of the event. Most will require a deposit up front. Be sure you clearly understand what is included in the contract.

Questions to ask a potential event planner include:

- How many charity events have you organized?
- Can you provide a list of references?
- Who will coordinate on the day of the event?
- Who is your contact person?
- Do they handle procuring other vendors as well? How is payment made to those vendors?
- How early do they need to start planning the event?
- Can they meet with staff and/or board members if necessary? Is meeting time included in the contract?
- Are they insured?
- How many events do they coordinate at a time?

Also, note if you still find yourself getting stressed out while planning your event, it is okay to step back and take a breather. In fact, throughout the entire planning period it is important that you make sure you are getting enough sleep, eating well, and treating yourself, in addition to planning ahead and preparing for the unexpected.

EVENT MARKETING

Marketing for your event is not limited to announcing that tickets are on sale and hoping the word spreads. In fact, there are so many options for marketing in today's world it can actually be overwhelming to choose which marketing route to take. From event websites to social media and everything in between, knowing how to market well can make or break an event.

Take the time to create a full marketing and development plan around your event and campaign. This needs to be done well in advance because when time gets tight and deadlines start appearing, the easiest thing to not get to is your marketing, which is ultimately going to heavily affect how many donors are in the room for your event.

Event Marketing includes promoting silent and live auction items, special speakers or guests, entertainers and emcees, and the cause itself. Your marketing plan should contain a combination of 12 or more "touches". These touches include direct mail (invitations, save the date) press and blog coverage, email, social media, phone calls, traditional media and digital media.

A key aspect to fundraising event marketing is preparing people to donate well before the event. Because of this, you need to be communicating with them about the mission and needs of the organization continually. You want your guests engaged with you and your cause before they even step foot in the door of the event.

Additionally, a significant aspect to running a successful non-profit organization with successful fundraising events is branding. Creating and maintaining a brand is essential to the mission, and having high visibility is necessary to maintaining a recognizable brand that people want to support. Utilizing your website, social media platforms, email and direct mailings coupled with personal contact will elevate your visibility. People want to be part of an organization that is accomplishing its goals. It's up to you to promote the message that yours is a progressive organization, and communicate that you want them to be part of the progress.

CREATE FOMO

FOMO (a.k.a. Fear Of Missing Out), will help drive your donors and sponsors to attend your main event. Nobody wants to miss out on a once-in-a-lifetime experience. After all, if you do a good job marketing your event, it will appear as if it is the event of the year which simply can't be missed. Be careful, however, not to over-inflate your event when marketing—you must deliver what you promise. By all means, present it as the event of the year. Don't however, state that it will be full of celebrities or sold out if you know this is not going to be the case. There's a fine line between creating a fear of missing out on an event and lying about what the event itself will actually be.

To create FOMO for your event, go out of your way to find items that would be unattainable outside of your auction (such as an autographed jersey from a beloved athlete, for example) and be sure to post about your rare find across all your chosen social media platforms. Additionally, make the event itself a destination with an activity or performance that guests could not get anywhere else. Be sure to promote this to the fullest so people know what to expect and can get excited. Finally, make it easy for others to share in the excitement across all social media platforms through simple links and hashtags. Build up anticipation by revealing new information about auction items and the event itself in the weeks leading up to the big night.

GETTING BUTTS IN THE SEATS

Getting the right people to your event is paramount to successful returns as we've already discussed. So think carefully about to whom and in what manner you are going to market. Again, consider what the purpose of your event is. To create awareness? Celebrate a milestone? Or primarily to raise money? Second, who is your audience going to be? Is there a specific age, geographic region, economic bracket or business category that makes the perfect, engaged donor/guest? All of these factors are important to consider when deciding on the marketing strategy you'll use for your event.

Below are some forms of marketing you might want to consider, as they tend to work well for fundraising events.

CREATING A WEBSITE

Your organization most likely has a website, but we strongly suggest also creating a website specifically for this event. This can be a microsite or subdomain of the organization's site. You can put a link to it on your main website page, but having a free-standing event website simplifies the user experience and is actually cheaper than paying a webmaster to change your master page to include all your event information and needs. By creating a website specifically for your event, you give your potential sponsors, donors and guests easy access to all the information they need. Additionally, it gives you one link to place in all social media, invitations, and emails, thus simplifying your marketing endeavors.

On your website, be sure to include:

- Event specifics such as: location, date, time, dress, and cost
- An event timeline
- Sponsor information (sponsor levels and benefits)
- Sponsor application
- If you are allowing vendors, a vendor application
- How to donate / get involved button or tab
- Purchase link
- Contact information (both email and phone number)
- Silent and live auction items as they come in
- Lists of any special events and/or guest speakers
- As this event is part of the branding and marketing of your organization, make sure you match the organization's colors, logo and branding guidelines, and dialogue.

SOCIAL MEDIA

Like it or not, social media is the main avenue by which many people communicate today. Therefore, effective event promotion will include a healthy social media component on a variety of platforms. Which platforms you utilize, however, are dependent upon your target audience, as well as the number of staff and volunteers you have. If your organization has social media platforms already established, utilize these to propagate your event followers. Invitations, direct messaging through various platforms, and sharing messages through board and committee members will multiply your messaging and "touches."

Use social media to post pictures of your cause and of your volunteers getting ready for the event. You can use last year's pictures to show people enjoying the festivities, post results from last year's gala, and show how your organization invested the money that was raised. Remember that video is king; short videos of the event—7 to 15 seconds each—can be shown on all social media platforms. Post stories about your cause or clientele, and don't forget testimonials. You can also post updates about new and exciting auction items that have come in, and of course, thank your sponsors as they come on board. In all cases, include graphics, photos or videos with your posts for maximum engagement.

Additionally, it is generally best if your social media team assigns one person the sole job of promoting the event on all your various social media platforms. This way, posting will be ensured on a regular basis and will be consistent. Ask your staff, board members, and volunteers to share event info on their own timelines. Tag people in photos, as this will cause it to show up in their feed as well, increasing visibility.

Generate "team" hashtags that are used by the board, staff, and volunteers for consistency. For example, if your event is the Saving the Animals Today Golf Tournament, shorten it to #statgolf2020. Then when anyone clicks on that hashtag, it will show every post made with that hashtag, which creates another place where people can go to find out about your event and organization.

EMAIL MARKETING

Your email database is the single most important marketing tool you have. After all, you have these names and emails because these people are already interested in your cause. In order to secure these mail addresses, however, it is important you have a mechanism to collect them on your website. This can be a "Join Our Newsletter" button or pop-up window. Also add a link and "Newsletter" button on your Facebook page. According to Blackbaud, a provider of online marketing and fundraising software, email is a highly effective marketing tool for nonprofits for several reasons:

1. It is cost-effective. Whereas direct mail can be extremely expensive, maintaining an email database is a very low-cost venture. Additionally, if you have a small organization, companies like MailChimp provide free newsletter tools.

2. You can use analytics. You can see within hours what percentage of recipients opened the email and even drill down into who specifically did or did not read it.

3. You can send personalized messages to different groups within your organization.

4. Email is immediate. You don't have to wait to go to print and then mail an announcement out. If you have an immediate need or an exciting announcement, it can go out in minutes.

5. You can use your email database to market your event by including information in your e-newsletter; by sending out e-blasts focused on a single story or message; a letter from the Executive Director, client, or board member; or an announcement or e-invite. Don't overwhelm your readers with too many emails. Email marketing should be part of a larger plan and integrated with your other marketing strategies.

6. Email can be shared by email list members to their friends and to social media platforms.

7. Respect the CAN-Spam Act and Terms of Service of the email service provider. Spamming is illegal and can result in

fines. Spamming is sending emails to anyone who did not "opt-in" or request to receive your email. See https://www.ftc.gov/tips-advice/business-center/guidance/can-spam-act-compliance-guide-business

PERSONAL PHONE CALLS

Nothing is more valuable than a personal invitation to an event. Reaching out to potential and previous donors is invaluable. It communicates they are valuable and their presence is desired. Before the call, be sure to verify what they have already invested in your cause in the past years. Then during the call, be sure to say "thank you" for their past help, offer a story about how their donation helped specifically, and inquire why they attended the event or donated in the past. This will help you learn about their values and what matters to them. If you are using donor software, be sure to capture this information in the notes for use in the future.

When you have them on the line, thank them for being a part of the mission and tell them about the exciting new things that have been going on. These phone calls are about developing a relationship that you want to last for the long-haul. If you are calling to market a specific event, be sure to convey your excitement about it and why it's worth their time to attend. Ask them to commit to coming and then direct them to where they can purchase their tickets. You can also offer to send them a direct personal link so they will be able to quickly register via a pre-filled out registration form online in addition to offering them a link they can share with those friends they may wish to have join them at the event. Furthermore, be sure to keep track of these phone calls in your donor software so you can follow up if you don't see the ticket purchase in the next few days.

DIRECT MAIL

Although more expensive than email or social media, direct mail has its place. Receiving a personal, professional invitation in the mail is very hard to put aside and forget about. Furthermore, it conveys the message that the people receiving the direct mailings are important. As we've said, there are so many organizations competing for donor dollars today, it's vital you let your supporters know they matter to you.

Points to consider about direct mailings:

- Choose the recipients carefully. Direct mail is expensive due to graphic design, printing, and postage; mass mailings generally do not work. Therefore, you must use your database as well as board and staff generated lists to get an idea of who should be on your list of mail recipients.

- Send a professionally designed and printed invitation.

- Follow up in two weeks with a phone call verifying that they received the invitation. Ask if they have any questions, and determine if they plan to attend.

CHAPTER 11
THE EVENT

Finally, the big day has arrived. You and your winning team have worked tirelessly for months, paying attention to every last detail to make this event one your donors will not want to miss. Everyone knows their part, the venue is decorated beautifully, the AV equipment has been tested, and the live and silent auction setups are ready to go. Everyone has their copy of the Run of Show Script, and you are completely prepared to pull off a spectacular event.

Now it's time to talk about the point of it all: maximizing the return on your investment so you can raise as much money as possible at the event. Let's talk about the art and science of *The Ask*—that pivotal moment when you ask your donors for their contribution to your cause.

The Ask, also known as the fund-a-need or special appeal, happens when you implore your guests to donate to a very specific need within your organization without receiving anything in return (apart from your gratitude and a feeling of being part of something larger than themselves, that is).

One of the most common questions we receive is, "Is it better to do The Ask before or after the live auction?" There are several ways to consider this decision.

There are advantages to doing The Ask first. By telling the story of the cause right out of the gate, your audience understands up front exactly what you're raising money for and why you are asking for gifts. This approach sets the tone from the very beginning. Most people that attend the event are there to give money. They show up with the intent of making a gift. FAN first events tend to be more for the well seasoned guest, with attendees that don't need or want 'stuff.'

Oftentimes, the donation/gifts come from the heart and the live auction purchases come from a place of fun. There are different ways to get into different checkbooks with different mindsets; we refer to this as the concept of a "Fun Money Account" versus a "Philanthropy Account." By putting The Ask first, you tap into the emotions of your guests and *then* free them to spend for fun.

Alternatively, you can conduct the live auction first and then have The Ask at the end. You may lean towards putting the live auction before the fund-a-need simply because the live auction can be fun, fast paced, high energy, and ego driven, lending itself to being completed before you ask people to partake in an empathetic, selfless Ask where you're asking them to give from the heart.

Some people will shop for the live auction items even before they come to the event, if given the opportunity. They will look at the program you send ahead of time with the list of items in the live auction. They're going to mentally shop and tally and come with a number already in mind that they will spend at the event. Everyone wants something for their dollar. The value of The Ask being at the end—after the Live Auction—is that if they didn't win their item, they will still spend the $3,500 that they had planned, and they will raise their paddle for that afterwards. If The Ask is first, they might not do that. They might say, *Oh, I'll give you $500 because I have to win this trip to Hawaii and I'm waiting to do that.*

The other factor at play is that people aren't paying full attention yet when they first sit down. They're drinking, talking with friends, viewing items in the silent auction, or might even be outside the reception altogether. Then, they come in and sit down to start the first course of the meal. Everyone in the room is chatting. You can't start by throwing an impact video up on the screen and believe that people are going to immediately stop what they're doing, start watching, and then bounce right into giving money. It's just not always enough time. People aren't prepared. Starting with the live auction is great, because it's energetic and loud, which mirrors the activity that is already happening in the room. When they hear the auctioneer's voice, people start to pay attention. They search for where he or she is standing, and they get caught up in how dynamic the whole show is. Then—at the very last live auction item, the auctioneer says, "Ladies and gentlemen, here's why we are here tonight." Start rolling the impact video, and it's magic.

THE DNA OF THE ASK

As we described earlier, there really is an art and science to The Ask. Now we are going to dive deeper into the details of setting up the right environment: we like to call this the DNA of The Ask.

1. The crowd should be seated at this point and ready to listen.

2. The room lights are down low and the lights are focused on the speaker.

   a. This doesn't need to be a spotlight. When there is a spotlight in the speaker's face, it is harder for them to see people and make that personal connection. Make sure that there is enough light for people to be able to see them, but dark enough so people understand that it's time to sit and listen.

3. There is value to having room for the person telling the story to walk around the room and make eye contact with those in the audience. If you are standing on stage the entire time, you are looking at the same few tables up front and it reduces your ability to make individual connections.

   a. You're not walking around and looking at everybody, you're picking your path strategically. You should know your seating plan and where some of your larger donors are sitting. Make sure you get out to those tables with purpose, but without looking like you're bee-lining toward and/or targeting them.

4. It's worth the investment to have a videographer connect live to screens around the event so that everyone can see and can focus on the speaker as they make their way around the

room. This can give each attendee the feeling that the speaker is talking directly to them, versus if they were on a stage far away the whole time.

5. Have a clear start and end time.

Floor Auctioneers/Ringmen/Spotters - During The Ask, if the auctioneer is walking around the room, he or she won't be able to see behind them. Have spotters there to watch when someone raises their hand in the back that your Auctioneer might not be able to see. Their job is to walk over to those guests, acknowledge they've been seen, alert the auctioneer, and let them know he or she will be on their way over to them. 90% of organizations have volunteers they can enroll to be spotters to assist with the live auction. The metric is to be prepared with one spotter for every 125 people in the crowd.

BE PREPARED

While The Ask is crucially important to the success of your event, there are a number of other things you need to be prepared for on the day of the event to ensure everything executes beautifully.

Donor Management

Seating arrangements are extremely important. You should know your guest list well enough to anticipate who the key people are that are going to raise their hand during the live auction or the appeal. Position those people around the room—if the larger donors are spread out, it challenges your guests from a fundraising perspective and encourages others to raise their paddles, as well.

Meet and Greet

Making your guests and donors feel appreciated and acknowledged is key to a Guest-Focused event. Assign each board member three tables to simply say "Thank you" to the guests seated there. It's challenging for the Executive Director to thank everyone personally in one evening, so this alleviates that pressure and ensures your guests all receive a face-to-face thank you.

Expect the Unexpected

Even the best laid plans can go awry, but being prepared for any crisis will alleviate the stress that inevitably comes with hiccups during your event. Use your professional judgement to remedy any situations that may arise and have a plan in place for some of the most common issues:

- Event is delayed
- Stolen items
- Bidder concerns
- Inebriated guests
- Missing volunteers

All of your months and months of hard work have led you to this event so remember to stay present and enjoy seeing the community come together in support of your organization!

CHAPTER 12
POST-EVENT

Your event is over, the evening has come to an end, and the night was just as successful as you'd hoped it would be. Now you're looking forward to some serious downtime.

But before you can take some time off, you'll need to tie up some loose ends to ensure everyone leaves with the proper impression and wants to return for your next event.

One of the questions we often get at our Eventology workshops is "With so many things to do following an event, what is the most important one to consider so that my attendees and donors are happy?"

It starts with who's on call the day after your event (often on a Sunday). No matter what day of the week it is, this day inevitably brings a list of post-event issues that arise. Overcharges, lost purse, buyer's remorse, and other things come up. You'll need to have a plan for who will field calls; even better would be to divide the day up into thirds and share the love (and phone duty) across a few key volunteers.

FINALIZING THE FINANCIALS

Within a few days of the event, you should ensure that each auction winner and Special Appeal donor has been appropriately charged for their purchases and donations. Credit card charges must be processed, checks deposited, and reports run (the type of reports you'll run will depend heavily on the type of software you are utilizing). Also be sure to email out receipts if they were not given out the night of the event.

Here are some report options you might consider:

- Grand total of all donations by type
- Total purchases/donations by guest
- Total purchases/donations by table
- How many guests donated the day of the event (% of attendees)

With this data, you can then complete the projected and actual budgets, and use this information to inform board members and staff about the success of the event. It is vital to look at post-event data in order to determine with whom you need to follow up, what auction items were the best sellers, which table hosts brought the most donors, and other important information. As stated in previous chapters, many organizations get caught up in the idea that more people at their event is better; however, after analyzing the data, it usually ends up surprising them when they realize how few people at their event actually donated. Knowing this information can prepare you and your board for the types of guests you want to curate for the following year and the types of auction items that are most sought after, thus increasing next year's revenue.

With your completed financial information you will also be able to determine your return on investment (ROI). For a fundraising dinner type event, the cost should be no higher than fifty cents on the dollar or 50%. This may sound high, but it is expensive to provide dinner and entertainment for guests. By preparing a final budget and determining the ROI, you have the ability to make focused decisions about what can be done at future events to lower costs and increase revenue.

TAKING CARE OF LOOSE ENDS

The week after the event can be exhausting. You may have many auction items that were not picked up, credit cards that were declined, and items that didn't sell.

Anticipate these follow-ups:

- Arranging for pick-up, delivery or shipment of items that were not picked up
- Issuance of certificates for consignment trips
- Deciding what to do with items that didn't sell. Do you donate them to another organization, sell them online or repackage them for another event?
- Follow-up with guests that may have needed special handling that evening and ensure their experience was a positive one.

THANK YOU, THANK YOU, THANK YOU!

This is the #1 job post-event. As soon as you can compile the information, each and every donor should be personally thanked with a phone call or a written thank you. This is where using event software can be a remarkable tool. With event management software, you should be able to run a report the next day identifying each donor, how much they gave, and in which area.

Suggestions for follow-up include:

- Divide the list into categories of major donors, mid-donors, and entry-level donors.

- Prior to the event, the team should decide who will thank whom. For example, perhaps board members make a personal phone call to all major donors, the Executive Director thanks the mid-level donors, and the development staff thanks everyone else.

- Follow up with a personally delivered thank you gift for sponsors and in-kind donors who donated high ticket items. This might be a pot of flowers planted by kids at the after school program, a signed picture by a family who has been helped, or a candy bouquet crafted by your staff. No matter what, it's the effort that matters here—nothing replaces face-to-face contact.

- Communicate results. With each phone call and visit, be sure to communicate how the funds will be used.

- Ask permission. Ask each donor for permission to place them on your email list if they aren't on it already. Tell them you want to keep them updated about how their valuable funds will be used to further the cause.

- Thank everyone. Send out a thank you to everyone who attended, whether they donated or not. Chances are, a portion of their ticket price is a donation. You want to cultivate that relationship. Even if they were there because someone gave them a ticket, it is possible they were moved by the story and are therefore a prospective donor.

- Ask for feedback. Send a post-event survey via email. When you speak with your donors, ask them what they enjoyed about the event and if they have any constructive feedback for next year.

YEAR-END DONOR APPRECIATION EVENT

An increasingly popular way to recognize donors is to hold a donor appreciation party or reception. You and your team can decide what level of donor will be invited and this may greatly depend upon the size of your organization. A small start-up nonprofit may choose to invite anyone who gave over $100, but a much larger, well-established organization might limit it to anyone who gave over $5,000. Donor thank you's can range from a barbecue to a cocktail reception to a luncheon. Evaluate what resources and contacts you have within your organization and how those might be utilized. If you have a board member who owns a winery, having a private barrel tasting would be a fantastic donor thank you. Or perhaps one of your key board members is an elected official; having a cocktail reception at his or her home will feel very exclusive to your donors.

We often hear from organizations that they "can't afford" donor parties or thank you gifts. The truth is, however, that you can't afford *not to* provide a memento of some kind. It is part of the cost of doing business. Put it in the event budget, and consider it an extension of the event itself. It is far less expensive to cultivate a relationship with a current donor than it is to develop a relationship with a new donor. By nurturing established sponsor relationships, your organization will experience higher giving over a longer period of time.

DON'T FORGET YOUR VOLUNTEERS!

Your volunteers are the backbone of your organization. Every person who gave their time for this event before, during, or after should be acknowledged. Just as we spoke earlier about donor fatigue, volunteer fatigue is a real thing, and it can be devastating if you're not careful. Good volunteers leave when they are overworked, take on too much work, or feel unappreciated. Just like donors, volunteers should be a priority and part of your stewardship plan. We would recommend putting this too into the budget and hosting a volunteer thank you party. It doesn't have to be fancy, but putting forth the effort to thank your volunteers means a great deal to them. Volunteers often become donors later; they are already clearly committed to the cause. Nurture and cultivate those relationships.

Creative ways to thank your volunteers:

- "Pay" your volunteers with a gift card provided by a sponsor in a handwritten thank you card.

- Volunteer happy hour/breakfast - ask a local hotspot to host a one hour happy hour/continental breakfast for the volunteers and acknowledge the event chairs and key volunteers.

- Invite volunteers to a board meeting and present them with a certificate of appreciation. This also makes for a great photo opportunity for local press.

DEBRIEFING

Having a debriefing session with stakeholders when the event is fresh in everyone's minds is an important part of event planning. It is ideal to have this scheduled before the event so everyone has it on their calendars. Be sure to invite anyone who was directly involved in the event, including committee members, staff, sponsors, key volunteers, and board members. Some organizations choose to invite key donors to the debriefing as well. This can be an excellent way to help donors feel integrally involved and start building the donor to funder relationship.

Items to discuss at your debriefing meeting:

- What went well: guest check-in, check-out, timing, speakers, flow of the evening, food, entertainment, centerpieces, audio-visual, volunteer assignments, auction items, software, technology, planning, etc.?
- What didn't go well?
- Feedback from stakeholders
- Metrics: The Development Director or the Executive Director should present metrics for the event, including:
  - The number of attendees and percentage of attendees who donated
  - Earned versus projected revenue
  - Categories of revenue and ROI on each
  - The live auction results including top item in terms of profit
  - The silent/online auction results

UPDATING THE DATABASE

In our daily interactions with charity organizations, we come across many groups that don't maintain donor databases in any organized fashion. Some depend on spreadsheets, paper records, or payment system records to track donor giving. We *strongly* suggest utilizing donor software. It allows you to maintain donor contact information, giving history, special information and requests, and event attendance. After the event ends, be sure to enter each new donor into the system and update existing donor profiles with any new information you captured at check-in. Data is the lifeblood of your organization, and if you can't reach your donor, chances are they won't reach you!

THE "OTHER" ASK
(NOT THE ONE YOU'RE THINKING OF)

We've talked a lot about "Making The Ask" and it's true that there is an art to it when you're meeting a prospective donor or sponsor for an event.

However, in our experience, that is not the most important Ask you'll make surrounding an event.

A lot of times we hear:

"Our board members are not engaged in fundraising"

"We have difficulty retaining donors and moving them up in their giving"

"We need to increase our volunteer base—we need more hands"

"Our event chair changes year over year, making it difficult to plan from scratch each year"

Ask your people what they think.

Yes, that is the ask: ask for their opinion. The power of engagement is a powerful tool.

Post-event surveys are popular, and while we do love them for gathering general feedback (food quality, auctioneer, check-in process, etc.), that's not enough.

ASKING BOARD MEMBERS

Do you have board members not engaged in fundraising? Dedicate half of the next board meeting to post-event feedback—the good the bad and the ugly. Some of the feedback you will be able to predict: the check out lines were too long, the chicken tasted like a shoe, etc. But we practically guarantee you will learn something that you never would have heard otherwise had you not asked. Even a small golden nugget of information can change the dynamic of a board and the participation of board members.

REAL LIFE EXAMPLE:

Roy, a developer, sits on a board supporting the athletic program at the middle and high schools in his town. He shows up to all of the meetings, votes on the minutes, chimes in when prompted, and that is about all.

Given the opportunity to provide feedback, he shared that the golf tournament had, in his opinion, been too focused on money. He and his friends are happy to come out and play golf but don't want to be asked at every hole for additional donations and suffer through a silent auction, raffle and live auction at the post golf dinner. The tournament committee asked him for suggestions to make it more golfer-friendly, which he happily provided. The discussion was lively and filled with many suggestions, and it ended with a solid game plan for the following year's event. After that meeting, not only did Roy offer to join the planning committee, he recruited five new teams to play and secured three hole sponsorships—including his own company for the first time. He was engaged.

ASKING DONORS

Do you have donors who don't return year after year, and if they do they give $100 bucks each year when you know they can give more?

Ask them why!

Here's a sample of a letter we sent to a donor.

Dear Jamie,

We are so appreciative of your donation last year [enter year]. We have built a new wing on the library, added daycare options for students and upgraded the computers throughout the college. We see that you haven't made a donation in two years and want to know if there is something we should know.

This is not a solicitation for money, but rather a request for genuine feedback.

Any suggestions would be much appreciated as we are striving to engage new donors and would love your advice for our future fundraising.

Thank you,

[Your signature]

Reaching out to key donors personally for feedback can have wildly positive results.

Here's another example:

One of the individuals I reached out to was a "large" event donor who was the type of person who liked to be the hero in the room. He had given about $10,000 at the last three years' events. I called to introduce myself and ask if he was going to be able to support us again.

"What did you like about last year's gala, and what do you think we could've done differently?" I asked.

Simply asking his opinion about the event itself turned into a long conversation about the band, the auctioneer, the food, the presentation, the wait staff, and the many things he did and did not like at the event.

I took diligent notes and later as we planned the event we took his opinion into consideration. Some of the things we didn't do: we didn't invite the local 30's style 10-piece orchestra to be the entertainment, for instance. But we *did* make sure the band was worthy of dancing to—both for a more mature crowd and for the younger guests—and we were certain not to have them play loud, live music during dinner.

Fast forwarding to the next year's event—he came up to me and said, "So it seems you liked my ideas?" I smiled and thanked him generously for his wonderful suggestions, and told him I hoped he enjoyed the evening.

Instead of his usual $10,000, he donated $30,000 that night and $40,000 the following year.

ASKING VOLUNTEERS

Volunteers RULE! We're serious—there is nothing better than a dedicated, passionate volunteer.

Want to know how to keep them engaged? Ask them for their opinion.

Ask them where to host the next event, get their opinion on what type of entertainment there should be, ask which golfers they would like to see at the golf tournament. Better yet, ask them for samples of something they've seen be successful at another event. Using their ideas (which, granted, doesn't always work) is powerful fuel for engagement. They will do more, connect others to the organization by recruiting their friends more, and donate more as a result of being asked what they think about the fundraising event.

The "Royalty" of the event, the volunteer Event Chair/Co-Chairs can really make an event. Often, they are the largest donor(s), they bring the most guests, recruit their personal friends to volunteer, secure most of the donations for the auctions, and more.

On the first day of planning the event, a lead staff member, board member and the event chair(s) sit around a circular table and Ask the chair(s) what they want for this event. They are asked for their vision—what their image of a successful night looks like. Ask them what details are most important to them.

The winning committee is one that is led by someone who feels their opinions are heard and whose ownership of the event is genuine.

Sometimes we don't want to ask for feedback because we might not want to hear the answers or we may be afraid that the ideas will be something we can't afford or fulfill. In our experience, both of those reasons are heavily outweighed by the value of The Ask. Sometimes we need to swallow our pride and if need be, discuss ideas a little more thoroughly to end in a solution that can be supported by all.

In all of the examples above, the common thread is trust. You are offering the opportunity to build trust with your board, with your donors and your volunteers. This trust is irreplaceable and will serve you well.

CONCLUSION

When we set out to write this book we had a few end goals in mind for you, our reader, to gain:

1. The confidence and flexibility to do events differently. To break out of the confines of traditional fundraising while making the donor and guest experience your organization's number one priority. In a sea of nonprofits, your focus on your people will be what differentiates you from the rest and sets you up for ongoing success.

2. Knowledge and access to expertise that you would then be able to share with fellow committee/board members. We believe passionately in newer concepts like collaborative fundraising and we want to see these innovative ideas spread far and wide. NPOs are designed to be the "helpers" in our society and as such, we want to see them thrive. Sharing

our personal experiences and knowledge seemed like a great place to start.

3. Increased credibility with your NPO in an effort to solidify your role as an effective leader and fundraiser in your organization. Learning to lead, knowing when to delegate, and discovering how to navigate the nonprofit world are all jobs in and of themselves. Our hope is that this book has given you the tools and resources to embrace your role within your organization.

4. The ability to raise more funds and create more impact for your constituents and beneficiaries. At the end of the day, fundraising is about generating revenue to create reach and impact. Every dollar raised and every donation given breathes life into your organization and furthers your mission. It sends kids to camp, it provides clean drinking water, it funds medical breakthroughs. Whatever your "WHY", nonprofit fundraising will better the lives of everyone involved.

It is our sincere hope that through this journey together we have achieved those four aims—and even perhaps a few more if we're lucky.

But the only way we'll know is to follow our own advice and make The Ask.

We would be honored if you would reach out to us to let us know what you learned, what your key takeaways were, and any things we could do to enhance the reader experience further or make this book better.

We look forward to having the opportunity to communicate with you directly and hope you'll either join us at an upcoming Eventology workshop, connect with us through social media, and/or send us an email to hello@fundraisingadvisors.org.

We're here to support your journey to nonprofit greatness, so please reach out if we can help you along that path in any way!

Darren & Michelle

ABOUT THE AUTHORS

DARREN DIESS

Darren Diess is a professional fundraising expert and advisor, donor development coach, and benefit auctioneer. He is one of only 3% of auctioneers nationwide to earn the Benefit Auctioneer Specialist designation. Darren's knowledge and experience in the fundraising world have helped nonprofits double or even triple their revenue and continue to receive donations long after the fundraising event is over. Founder of Strategic Fundraising Solutions and an AFP Board member, Darren knows that volunteer, amateur, and celebrity auctioneers often leave money in the room. His focus is on high-impact auction fundraising for 501(c)(3) charitable organizations.

When Darren isn't onstage or planning his next auction, he enjoys spending time in the San Diego sunshine with his lovely wife and three adult children.

MICHELLE GILMORE

Michelle Gilmore speaks nonprofit. Starting her career in education she has come full circle with her Eventology classes, workshops and trainings. She graduated from Arizona State University with a Bachelor of Science in Sociology, earned her California teaching credential from National University and a Masters of Arts in Education in Curriculum Development from San Diego State University. Following ten years of teaching, Michelle put her passion for volunteering and fundraising to work raising funds for arts and music programs for public schools. Teaching Art as a volunteer, hosting multiple fundraising events from galas to 10K races, carnivals to talent shows, Michelle merged her education-focused background with fundraising savvy to make a difference. From auction basket coordinator to Board President, Michelle has held positions on multiple boards, coached fellow nonprofits on maximizing revenue at their events, and eventually re-entered the workforce as a Development Officer for a local Schools Foundation. Through her work at the Foundation and her current role as Senior Development Director at the Cystic Fibrosis Foundation, Michelle has raised millions of dollars for non-profit organizations and earned her CFRE certification in 2019.

Michelle and her husband, Ted, have three boys and live in Coronado, California. She still volunteers for arts and education nonprofit organizations and sits on the board of a local non-profit that funds buses for public school field trips.

GLOSSARY

Auction Walk - This is when the auctioneer begins with the first item in a silent auction. Then when he or she reaches each item, the item closes and the highest bidder for that item wins it.

Benefit Auctioneer Specialist (BAS) - A professional auctioneer trained specifically for fundraising auctions and certified by the NAA - National Association of Auctioneers.

Bidder Numbers - Pre-assigned numbers for each guest at your live event, usually printed on stickers and paddles to make it easy for guests to bid on items.

Consignment Items - Items provided to your event by consignment vendors that are considered unique and/or rare for which a minimum price must be met in order to be sold and a reserve fee must be paid.

Crowdfunding - Operating on the principle "it takes a village," organizations or even individual people can post a project or cause on a crowdfunding website and donors will then contribute to the cause they choose.

All or Nothing (AoN) - A crowdfunding campaign in which your organization must meet its financial goal in order to keep the funds it has raised via that particular crowdfunding campaign.

Keep it All (KIA) - A crowdfunding campaign in which your organization may keep all the funds raised during that particular campaign, regardless of whether the goal is reached or not.

Customer and Client Relationship Management Software (CRMS) - Software used to keep track of customers and donors.

Donors - People or organizations who donate money to your cause, either on a one-time or recurring basis.

Donor to Funder Relationship - Similar to the Sponsor to Funder Relationship, Donor to Funder relationships involve a donor who becomes increasingly more involved within your organization, acting as more than just a donor.

Estate Giving - A long-time (or short-time) supporter of your cause bequeathing your organization their estate upon their death.

Event Management Software (EMS) - Software utilized by a company and/or nonprofit to keep track of all information for their event, as well as to check guests in/out, run credit cards, store bidder information, and more.

Endowment - An endowment is a donation of money or property to a non-profit organization, which uses the resulting investment income for a specific purpose.

FOMO - Fear Of Missing Out on an event of a lifetime.

Giving Day - A day which aims to bring people together to solve local and international challenges through generous giving.

Payment Card Industry (PCI) - A company that sets levels of credit card transaction security.

Peer-to-Peer Fundraising - A single cause fundraising vehicle in which individuals are asked to donate utilizing a social media platform, however, supporters directly reach out to their own personal network of friends, family, and business associates to personally ask them to participate in the cause versus creating an entire advertising campaign for strangers.

Planned Giving - This type of giving involves any type of giving to your organization by individuals in which plans for that act of giving need to be made in advance (like estate giving for example).

Procurement Packet - A short letter to give your potential sponsors which explains who your organization is, what it does and acts as a voucher for your tax exempt status as well as a sort of receipt for said sponsors, should they end up supporting your cause.

Professional Floor Auctioneers - Also called "Bid Spotters," these are professional auctioneers which roam the floor during the live auction, helping to raise bids as well as spot bids the main auctioneer may overlook in the crowd.

Recurring Giving - Donors who opt to give a specified amount each month as opposed to a one-time donation.

Reserves - The money your organization has set aside to keep itself running in the event of a slow funding year.

Return on Investment (ROI) - The money and benefit you get back from your event thanks to your initial investment of both money and time.

Run of Show - From event setup through the tear-down, the Run of Show is the written document that explains to the 'behind-the-scenes' organizers the detailed sequence of events planned. It is the master document that contains all the critical components of the event.

Special Appeal - also known as the "fund-a-need", "fund-a-cause" or the "paddle raise", is the moment in the night where you ask your guests to participate in a specific cause related to your organization to help support your mission.

Sponsors - Also called Underwriters, are people who will give money or products to your organization, specifically to help fund the cost of your event (though they may wish to donate funds to your charity as well). In return for this, sponsors will generally receive some sort of advertising and marketing at your event in return.

Sponsor Activation - Refers to the manner in which you engage the sponsor's brands.

Sponsor to Funder Vision - Support from a single donor all year long, both financially and in the form of time and help, thus turning them into a founder instead of just a sponsor or donor.

Spotters - See Professional Floor Auctioneers.

Underwriters - See Sponsors.

Vendors - Companies and/or people your organization hires to help put on your event (e.g. caterers, event planners, auctioneers, entertainment, etc).

Workplace Giving - A type of giving which involves making a deal with a company who has agreed to offer their employees the opportunity to donate either funds or volunteer hours to your organization.